Death
and
Responsibility

SUNY series in Contemporary Continental Philosophy
Dennis J. Schmidt, Editor

Death
and
Responsibility

The "Work" of Levinas

Dennis King Keenan

State University of New York Press

Published by
State University of New York Press, Albany

© 1999 State University of New York

For information, address State University of New York Press,
State University Plaza, Albany, N.Y. 12246

Production by E. Moore
Marketing by Anne Valentine

Library of Congress Cataloging-in-Publication Data

Keenan, Dennis King, 1960–
    Death and responsibility : the "work" of Levinas / Dennis King
Keenan.
        p.   cm. — (SUNY series in contemporary continental
philosophy)
    Includes bibliographical references and index.
    ISBN 0-7914-4077-X (alk. paper). — ISBN 0-7914-4078-8 (pbk. :
alk. paper)
    1. Lévinas, Emmanuel. 2. Responsibility. 3. Death. I. Title.
II. Series.
B2430.L484K43 1999
194—dc21   98-24165
                                                                          CIP

10 9 8 7 6 5 4 3 2 1

for Liz

Contents

Acknowledgments

This work was made possible, in part, by a summer research stipend from Fairfield University. Portions of this work have appeared earlier in altered form in journals: a portion of chapter 1 appeared as "Reading Levinas Reading Descartes' *Meditations*," in *The Journal of the British Society for Phenomenology*, 29 (1998), W. Mays, editor; a portion of chapter 2 appeared as "Skepticism and the Blinking Light of Revelation," in *Epoché: A Journal for the History of Philosophy*, 4 (1996), James E. Faulconer, editor; and a portion of chapter 5 appeared as "Responsibility and Death," in *Philosophy Today*, 42 (1998), David Pellauer, editor. I am grateful to the editors for permission to use these materials here.

Portions of Levinas's *Totality and Infinity* are used with kind permission of Duquesne University Press: Emmanuel Levinas, *Totality and Infinity: An Essay on Exteriority*. Translated by Alphonso Lingis. Pittsburgh: Duquesne University Press, 1969. Portions of Levinas's *Otherwise than Being* are used with kind permission of Kluwer Academic Publishers: Emmanuel Levinas, *Otherwise than Being or Beyond Essence*. Translated by Alphonso Lingis. The Hague: Martinus Nijhoff, 1981. The background of the cover is used with kind permission of Kluwer Academic Publishers: Emmanuel Levinas, *Totalité et Infini: Essai sur l'extériorité*, 4th ed. The Hague: Martinus Nijhoff, 1984, p. 25.

Many thanks to Rene McGraw, who sparked the flame of philosophical wonder in me, and to John Sallis, Robert Bernasconi, Paul Davies, Tom Sheehan, and John Llewelyn, who nurtured that flame. Thanks also to Dave Livingston, Travis Anderson, and Randy Honold, companions on the way, and to Paul Lakeland and Kathi Weeks, who helped bring this book to completion. Finally, a special thanks to Liz, to whom this book is dedicated.

Abbreviations

WORKS BY EMMANUEL LEVINAS

AE/OB   *Autrement qu'être ou au-delà de l'essence*. Dordrecht: Kluwer, 1991 / *Otherwise than Being or Beyond Essence*. Translated by Alphonso Lingis. The Hague: Martinus Nijhoff, 1981.

AV/BV   *L'au-delà du verset: Lectures et discours talmudiques*. Paris: Minuit, 1982 / *Beyond the Verse: Talmudic Readings and Lectures*. Translated by Gary D. Mole. Bloomington: Indiana University Press, 1994.

DEE/EE   *De l'existence à l'existant*. Paris: Vrin, 1990 / *Existence and Existents*. Translated by Alphonso Lingis. The Hague: Martinus Nijhoff, 1978.

DEL   "Dialogue with Emmanuel Levinas." Translated by Richard Kearney. In *Face to Face with Levinas*, 13–33. Edited by Richard A. Cohen. Albany: State University of New York Press, 1986.

DL/DF   *Difficile liberté: Essais sur le judaïsme*, 2nd ed. Paris: Albin Michel, 1963 and 1976 / *Difficult Freedom: Essays on Judaism*. Translated by Seán Hand. Baltimore: The Johns Hopkins University Press, 1990.

DP/GP   "Dieu et la philosophie." In *De Dieu qui vient à l'idée*, 2nd ed., 93–127. Paris: Vrin, 1992 / "God and Philosophy." Translated by Alphonso Lingis and Richard Cohen. In *Emmanuel Levinas: Collected Philosophical Papers*, 153–173. Dordrecht: Martinus Nijhoff, 1987.

MT   *La mort et le temps*. Paris: Éditions de l'Herne, 1991.

NSS   "Notes sur le sens." In *De Dieu qui vient à l'idée*, 2nd ed., 231–57. Paris: Vrin, 1992.

PeI/PaI   "La philosophie et l'idée de l'Infini." In *En découvrant l'existence avec Husserl et Heidegger*, 165–78. Paris: Vrin, 1967 / "Philosophy and the Idea of Infinity." Translated by Alphonso Lingis. In *Emmanuel Levinas: Collected Philosophical Papers*, 47–59. Dordrecht: Martinus Nijhoff, 1987.

SI/US   "La souffrance inutile." In *Les Cahiers de La nuit surveillée, Numéro 3; Emmanuel Levinas*, 329–38. Edited by Jacques Rolland. Paris: Éditions Verdier, 1984 / "Useless Suffering." Translated by Richard Cohen. In *The Provocation of Levinas: Rethinking the Other*, 156–67. Edited by Robert Bernasconi and David Wood. London: Routledge, 1988.

SS/MS   "La signification et le sens." In *Humanisme de l'autre homme*, 15–70. Montpellier: Fata Morgana, 1972 / "Meaning and Sense." Translated by Alphonso Lingis. In *Emmanuel Levinas: Collected Philosophical Papers*, 75–107. Dordrecht: Martinus Nijhoff, 1987.

SS/NTR   *Du sacré au saint: Cinq nouvelles lectures talmudiques*. Paris: Minuit, 1977 / *From the Sacred to the Holy: Five New Talmudic Readings*. In *Nine Talmudic Readings*, 89–197. Translated by Annette Aronowicz. Bloomington: Indiana University Press, 1990.

TA/TO   *Le temps et l'autre*. Paris: PUF, 1991 / *Time and the Other*. Translated by Richard A. Cohen. Pittsburgh: Duquesne University Press, 1991.

TdA/ToO   "La trace de l'autre." In *En découvrant l'existence avec Husserl et Heidegger*, 187–202. Paris: Vrin, 1967 / "The Trace of the Other." Translated by Alphonso Lingis. In *Deconstruction in Context: Literature and Philosophy*, 345–59. Edited by Mark C. Taylor. Chicago: University of Chicago Press, 1986.

TdI/ToI   *Théorie de l'intuition dans la phénoménologie de Husserl*, 5th ed. Paris: Vrin, 1984 / *The Theory of Intuition in Husserl's Phenomenology*. Translated by André Orianne. Evanston: Northwestern University Press, 1973.

TeI/TaI   *Totalité et Infini: Essai sur l'extériorité*, 4th ed. The Hague: Martinus Nijhoff, 1984 / *Totality and Infinity: An Essay on Exteriority*. Translated by Alphonso Lingis. Pittsburgh: Duquesne University Press, 1969.

TM/TE   "Transcendance et Mal." In *De Dieu qui vient à l'idée*, 2nd ed., 189–207. Paris: Vrin, 1992 / "Transcendence and Evil." Translated by Alphonso Lingis. In *Emmanuel Levinas: Collected Philosophical Papers*, 175–86. Dordrecht: Martinus Nijhoff, 1987.

OTHER WORKS

AM/AD   Jacques Derrida, *Apories: Mourir—s'attendre aux «limites de la vérité.»* In *Le passage des frontières: Autour du travail de Jacques Derrida*, 309–38. Paris: Galilée, 1994 / *Aporias: Dying—Awaiting (One Another at) the "Limits of Truth."* Translated by Thomas Dutoit. Stanford: Stanford University Press, 1993.

ASZ/TSZ   Friedrich Nietzsche, *Also sprach Zarathustra: Ein Buch für Alle und Keinen.* In *Werke: Kritische Gesamtausgabe*, Abt. VI, Bd. 1. Edited by Giorgio Colli and Mazzino Montinari. Berlin: Walter de Gruyter, 1968 / *Thus Spoke Zarathustra: A Book for All and None.* Translated by Walter Kaufmann. New York: Penguin, 1978.

CD/IC   Jean-Luc Nancy, *La communauté désœuvrée.* Paris: Christian Bourgois Editeur, 1986 / *The Inoperative Community.* Translated by Peter Connor, Lisa Garbus, Michael Holland, and Simona Sawhney. Minneapolis: University of Minnesota Press, 1991.

CI/UC   Maurice Blanchot, *La communauté inavouable.* Paris. Munuit, 1983 / *The Unavowable Community.* Translated by Pierre Joris. Barrytown, New York: Station Hill Press, 1988.

DG/OG   Jacques Derrida, *De la grammatologie*. Paris: Minuit, 1967 / *Of Grammatology*. Translated by Gayatri Chakravorty Spivak. Baltimore: Johns Hopkins University Press, 1976.

DM/GD   Jacques Derrida, *Donner la mort*. In *L'éthique du don, Jacques Derrida et la pensée du don*, 11–108. Paris: Métailié-Transition, 1992 / *The Gift of Death*. Translated by David Wills. Chicago: University of Chicago Press, 1995.

ED/WD   Maurice Blanchot, *L'écriture du désastre*. Paris: Gallimard, 1980 / *The Writing of the Disaster*. Translated by Ann Smock. Lincoln: University of Nebraska Press, 1986.

EeD/WaD   Jacques Derrida, *L'écriture et la différence*. Paris: Seuil, 1967 / *Writing and Difference*. Translated by Alan Bass. Chicago: University of Chicago Press, 1978.

EI/IC   Maurice Blanchot, *L'entretien infini*. Paris: Gallimard, 1969 / *The Infinite Conversation*. Translated by Susan Hanson. Minneapolis: University of Minnesota Press, 1993.

EL/SL   Maurice Blanchot, *L'espace littéraire*. Paris: Gallimard, 1955 / *The Space of Literature*. Translated by Ann Smock. Lincoln: University of Nebraska Press, 1982.

FB/FT   Søren Kierkegaard, *Frygt og Bœven: Dialektisk Lyrik*. In *Søren Kierkegaards Samlede Værker*, vol. III. Edited by A. B. Drachman, J. L. Heiberg, and H. O. Lange. Copenhagen: Gyldendal, 1901–06 / *Fear and Trembling: Dialectical Lyric*. Edited and Translated by Howard V. Hong and Edna H. Hong. Princeton: Princeton University Press, 1983.

GdM/GoM   Friedrich Nietzsche, *Zur Genealogie der Moral: Eine Streitschrift*. In *Werke: Kritische Gesamtausgabe*, Abt. VI, Bd. 2. Edited by Giorgio Colli and Mazzino Montinari. Berlin: Walter de Gruyter, 1968 / *On the Genealogy of Morals: A Polemic*. Translated by Walter Kaufmann. New York: Random House, 1967.

LDM/LRD   Maurice Blanchot, "La littérature et le droit à la mort." In *La part du feu*, 291–331. Paris: Gallimard, 1949 / "Literature and the Right to Death." Translated by Lydia Davis. In *The Gaze of Orpheus*, 21–62. Edited by P. Adams Sitney. Barrytown, New York: Station Hill Press, 1981.

MpP/MfP Jacques Derrida, *Mémoires pur Paul de Man*. Paris: Galilée, 1988 / *Memoires for Paul de Man*. Translated by Cecile Landsay, Jonathan Culler, and Eduardo Cadava. New York: Columbia University Press, 1986.

MPP/MFP René Descartes, *Meditationes de prima philosophia*. In *Oeuvres de Descartes*, vol. VII, 1–90. Edited by Charles Adam and Paul Tannery. Paris: Vrin, 1983 / *Meditations on First Philosophy*. Translated by John Cottingham. In *The Philosophical Writings of Descartes*, vol. II, 1–62. Cambridge: Cambridge University Press, 1988.

NF/WP Friedrich Nietzsche, *Nachgelassene Fragmente*. In *Werke: Kritische Gesamtausgabe*, Abt. VIII, Bd. 1. Edited by Giorgio Colli and Mazzino Montinari. Berlin: Walter de Gruyter, 1974 / *The Will to Power*. Translated by Walter Kaufmann and R. J. Hollingdale. New York: Random House, 1967.

P Jacques Derrida, *Points . . . : Interviews, 1974–1994*. Translated by Peggy Kamuf & others. Edited by Elisabeth Weber. Stanford: Stanford University Press, 1995.

PG/PS G. W. F. Hegel, *Phänomenologie des Geistes*. Edited by Wolfgang Bonsiepen and Reinhard Heede. In *Gesammelte Werke*, Bd. 9. Hamburg: Felix Meiner Verlag, 1980 / *Phenomenology of Spirit*. Translated by A. V. Miller. Oxford: Oxford University Press, 1977.

PHE/SHE Jean Wahl, *Petite histoire de "l'existentialisme."* Paris: Éditions Club Maintenant, 1947 / *A Short History of Existentialism*. Translated by Forrest Williams and Stanley Maron. New York: Philosophical Library, 1949.

SZ/BT Martin Heidegger, *Sein und Zeit*, 9th ed. Tübingen: Max Niemeyer, 1960 / *Being and Time*. Translated by John Macquarrie and Edward Robinson. New York: Harper & Row, 1962.

TCU/TCD Jan Patočka, "Je technická civilizace úpadková, a proč?" In *Kacířské eseje o filosofii dějin*, 105–26. Praha: Academia, 1990 / "Is Technological Civilization Decadent, and Why?" Translated by Erazim Kohák. In *Heretical Essays in the Philosophy of History*, 95–118. Edited by James Dodd. Chicago: Open Court, 1996.

Introduction

For the most part, the work of Levinas has been too easily read. Levinas's use of words such as *responsibility* and *God* gives some readers reason to dismiss his work as insufficiently attentive to the whispered suspicions of our times, while giving others reason to accept his work as a clarion call guiding them out of this wilderness of disorienting whispers. My reading of death in the work of Levinas frustrates both this ready dismissal and this ready acceptance.

The radicality of Levinas's work is evident when it is situated within the context of other readings of death. In Hegel, death traditionally has been read as a necessary moment in the progression of Spirit through the different forms of consciousness to absolute knowing. For Hegel, death is productive. It is the effectuation of the appearance of the next shape of the dialectic. In Nietzsche, as well, death is the possibility of the step beyond. The overman, as the one free for the possibility of death, as the one who maintains the pure essence of will in willing nothingness, is the decisive step beyond the nihilism of *ressentiment*, the bad conscience, and the ascetic ideal. In Heidegger, the authentic, resolute, determinate, and decided assumption of death is the step that would complete the existential analysis of Dasein.

Levinas, however, has articulated (along with Derrida and Blanchot) an irreducible ambiguity at the heart of death. This reading acknowledges (though not always with explicit reference to Hegel's or Nietzsche's work) the power of death, while, at the same time, exposing the powerlessness of death. This reading of death (though not in every case is it a reading explicitly produced by Levinas) exposes that *moment* when death as possibility turns into death as impossibility, that is, turns into death as the impossibility of dying, the impossibility (within a Hegelian context) of producing the progressive steps of the dialectic, the impossibility (within a Nietzschean context) of effecting the decisive step of the overman, and finally, the impossibility (within a Heideggerian context) of the step that completes the existential analysis of Dasein. Here one sees a step beyond that is, *at the same time*, not beyond. Here one sees the ruination of a step *in the performance of the step itself*. Here one sees the unworking of the "work." Levinas refers to this *moment* of the interruption of the "work" as *le temps mort*, "dead time," which is a colloquial French phrase that refers to time wasted, an idle period (in a movement), an interruption. A comparable colloquial phrase in English might be *down time*.

This reading has profound consequences for those readers of Levinas mentioned earlier, who too readily dismiss or accept his work, based on his use of the word *responsibility*. For example, in Levinas's work responsibility must, I would suggest, be read alongside death, which in turn, I would further suggest, calls for it being read alongside the work of Derrida and Blanchot. What responsibility requires is "given" by the aporia of death. Derrida points out that responsibility requires that I respond, that I answer for what I do, say, and give, as irreplaceable singularity, *and* it requires that I am exposed to ex-propriation, to anonymity, that I forget or efface myself, that I be (in Levinas's words) nothing but "for the Other." In other words, responsibility requires—using words of Blanchot that echo Heidegger's analysis of death as possibility of the impossibility of Dasein—that I answer for the impossibility of being responsible, which makes me always already irresponsible or guilty. The more I am responsible, the more irresponsible I am, because (on the one hand) responsibility holds *me* accountable, and (on the other hand) responsibility *discounts* me (insofar as it requires that I be *selfless*). Only the aporia of death—that moment when death as possibility turns into death as impossibility—is adequate to the aporia of responsibility, insofar as death as possibility gives irreplaceable singularity and death as impossibility gives the ex-propriation, the anonymity, that is a forgetting or effacement of oneself.

This book begins with Levinas's reading of Descartes' *Meditations on First Philosophy*. Descartes' *Meditations* plays a major role in Levinas's work. The profundity of the *Meditations* lies, for Levinas, in "[t]he ambiguity of Descartes's first evidence, revealing the I and God in turn without merging them, revealing them as two distinct moments of evidence mutually founding one another" (TeI 19/TaI 48). Levinas is also attentive to another ambiguity in Descartes' work: the incessant alternation between doubt and refutation of doubt that is a spiraling movement of descent toward an ever more profound abyss that Levinas calls *il y a* and associates with the evil genius. The performance of these ambiguities is, I would suggest, a "drama in several acts" (TeI 258/TaI 282; see also TeI 260/TaI 284). What is produced in these performances is not something that appears unambiguously, but rather an irreducible ambiguity, a trace of what infinitely approaches (or withdraws from) revelation, of what is "not yet." It is a production of a trace of the not yet of the subject and the not yet of the other. The performance of these two movements is the production of a trace of the subject *as* interrupted and the other *as* interrupting. It is the production of a trace of what Levinas calls "dead time." Here one sees a productionless production. Here one sees the ruination of the "work" *in the performance of the work itself.* Here one sees a performance of the unworking of the work that is re-enacted throughout Levinas's work.

This reading is sustained throughout my work (as well as Levinas's) and as such provides a familiar point of departure and return for a reader negotiating the work of Levinas for the first time. As was suggested earlier, however, this familiar point of departure and return is not as comforting as it may at first seem. There is an unworking at the heart of the work of Descartes' *Meditations.* As such, it is a profoundly disturbing work, whose effects are felt throughout Levinas's work.

For example, those readers of Levinas mentioned earlier, who either readily dismiss his work or readily accept it, based on his use of the word *God,* will have their too easy reading frustrated. According to the "logic" of this reading, God (the infinite) is not someone or something with which I am in an unambiguous relation. The phrase *relation without relation* is used by Levinas to articulate the fact that one term of the relation (that is, God) absolves itself from the relation, or said otherwise, merely leaves a trace of itself in the irreducibly ambiguous double origin of God and the subject that Levinas reads alongside his work on skepticism. God merely leaves a trace of itself in what Levinas calls the "blinking light" of a double origin or incessant alternation. God, according to Levinas, is not revealed (or concealed) unambiguously. Neither simply present nor simply absent, God infinitely approaches (or withdraws from) revelation. Therefore, the relation without relation is an *à-Dieu*—an interminable approach of or going *to God* that is at the same time an interminable withdrawal or *good-bye.* God "is" only as approach (or withdrawal). God is only *as* the interruption of the isolated subject, which for Levinas is the beginning of responsibility.

The disturbing effects of these readings of responsibility and God are compounded in a reading of the work of Levinas alongside Genesis 22 (by way of the work of Derrida). Here the couple responsibility/irresponsibility is considered not only with respect to the asymmetrical relationship of the self and the other, but also with respect to the relationship of the self with the other others. Genesis 22 shows that in the singular relationship with the singular other (the infinite), which *already* involves irresponsibility, one is inevitably implicated in *another* form of irresponsibility—the sacrifice of the other other, the others other than God.

Genesis 22, the story of the binding (the *Akedah*) of Isaac, shows that in every authentic decision the ethical *has* to be sacrificed. The binding produces a double bind. God summons Abraham to absolute responsibility. Absolute responsibility binds Abraham in his absolute irreplaceability to God as the name of the absolute other as other and as unique. But to respond to God is to sacrifice every other other to whom Abraham should be bound; it is to sacrifice what Kierkegaard in *Fear and Trembling* calls the "ethical order." Absolute responsibility requires that one behave in an irresponsible manner, while still belonging to and recognizing what is sacrificed.

The aporia of responsibility is complicated by the formula *tout autre est tout autre*, every other (one) is every (bit) other, which disturbs Kierkegaard's discourse on the absolute uniqueness of Jahweh while pushing it to its logical conclusion, because it implies that the wholly other God is everywhere one finds the wholly other. God—serving as the index not only of the *wholly other* (*tout autre*) but also of *every* (other) *other* (*tout autre*)—is other than himself; God is his "own" other.

The ambiguity of the word *à-Dieu* serves to gather together many of the ideas considered in the book. In absolute responsibility a going *to God* and a *good-bye* coincide: *à-Dieu*. This "good-bye" of/to God has several different (are they different?) trajectories: (1) good-bye of/to God as palpably present insofar as God is absent, hidden and silent, separate, secret, at the moment that God has to be obeyed, (2) good-bye of/to God as transcendent insofar as God becomes its own other, becomes finite, becomes incarnated as command, with the self thereby becoming its own other, and (3) good-bye of/to God as transcendent guarantee of the Good, of responsibility, insofar as God becomes its own other, that is, the demonic, the *il y a*. The *à-Dieu* marks the aporia that responsibility *has* to be transgressed *in the name of* an absolute obligation to God, which merely serves as an index not only of the *wholly other* (*tout autre*) but also of *every* (other) *other* (*tout autre*). The *à-Dieu* marks the moment when a linear movement oriented in the direction of a goal, a production, a work, finds itself at a distance from itself, is interrupted.

Chapter 1

The Infinite and the Evil Genius:
Reading Descartes' *Meditations on First Philosophy*

Descartes' *Meditations on First Philosophy* plays a major role in Levinas's work. The profundity of the *Meditations* lies, for Levinas, in "[t]he ambiguity of Descartes's first evidence, revealing the I and God in turn without merging them, revealing them as two distinct moments of evidence mutually founding one another" (TeI 19/TaI 48). This ambiguous "double origin"[1] of the *cogito* and the infinite is performed in a reading that progresses from the First Meditation to the discovery of the infinite in the Third Meditation. This performance of what I would suggest is a "drama in several acts" (TeI 258/TaI 282; see also TeI 260/TaI 284) is the production of a trace of the *infinition* of the infinite, of the infinite *as* interrupting the thought that thinks it. This performance is re-enacted throughout Levinas's work.

However, the role played by Descartes' *Meditations* in Levinas's work is not limited to the performance of the double origin of the *cogito* and the infinite. Levinas also reads the performance of an irreducible double movement into Descartes' presentation of the evil genius.

The performance of these two irreducible double movements not only interrupts a traditional reading of Descartes' *Meditations*, but also interrupts a too easy reading of Levinas's work.

Prior to 1957 there are a few scattered references by Levinas to the work of Descartes. "Philosophy and the Idea of Infinity," published in 1957, introduces a reading of the Cartesian analysis of the idea of infinity that will play either an explicit or an implicit role in most of Levinas's subsequent work, most obviously in the very title of the work *Totality and Infinity*. In Descartes' *Meditations*, Levinas finds an I that thinks, which maintains a relationship with the infinite in which the alterity of the infinite is not "extinguished" by the thought that thinks it. "In thinking infinity the I from the first *thinks more than it thinks*" (PeI 172/PaI 54). This aporetic formulation is, I would suggest, elaborated in *Totality and Infinity* in terms of two contradictory movements that necessarily yet impossibly call for being thought together. It is important to note that even in its introduction in "Philosophy and the Idea of Infinity" Levinas's reading of Descartes' *Meditations* retains "only the *formal* design of the structure it outlines" (PeI 171/PaI 53). The two movements are an elaboration of this "formal design" of the *Meditations* that fascinates Levinas. "If, in a first movement, Descartes takes a consciousness to be indubitable of itself by itself, in a second movement—the reflection on reflection—he recognizes conditions for this certitude" (TeI 186/TaI 210). Before undertaking a close textual reading of Levinas's reading of Descartes' *Meditations* it is necessary to situate these two movements within the context of the distinction Levinas makes between comprehension and critique.

In the opening sections of *Totality and Infinity* Levinas makes a distinction between knowledge or theory understood as comprehension and the critical essence of knowing. In its comprehension of being, knowledge or theory is concerned with critique. Discovering the arbitrary dogmatism of its free exercise, knowing calls itself into question. The critical essence of knowing turns back at every moment to the origin of this arbitrary dogmatism of its free exercise (TeI 13/TaI 43). The essence of knowing does not consist in grasping an object, but in being able to call itself into question. Knowing "can have the world as its theme, make of it an object, because its exercise consists, as it were, in taking charge of the very condition that supports it and that supports even this very act of taking charge" (TeI 57/TaI 85). Knowledge or theory seems, therefore, to be characterized by an ambiguity—two distinct movements. The movement of comprehension is inverted at every moment by the movement of critique. However, these two movements are not *merely* opposed to one another. Although oriented in inverse directions, and therefore opposed, they nevertheless call for being thought at the same time. "Knowing becomes knowing of a fact only if it is *at the same time [en même temps]* critical, if it puts itself into question, goes back beyond its origin—in an unnatural movement to seek higher than one's own origin, a movement which evinces or describes a created freedom" (TeI 54/TaI 82–83, emphasis added). In this unnatural movement of critique, knowledge goes back beyond its *own* origin, that is, back beyond an origin in which it is justified by itself. "Knowledge as a critique, as a tracing back to what precedes freedom, can arise only in a being that has an origin prior to its origin—that is created" (TeI 57/TaI 85). The moment when comprehension is called into question by critique is what Levinas calls "ethics" or "morality." This suggests, as Robert Bernasconi has noted, "that the ambitions of epistemology are only fulfilled when it recognizes itself as morality."[2] Levinas discovers this ambiguous double movement, and therefore an "ethical" structure, in Descartes' *Meditations on First Philosophy*.

The critical essence of knowing leads—according to Levinas's reading of Descartes' *Meditations*—beyond the knowledge of the *cogito* (TeI 58/TaI 85). It penetrates beneath knowledge understood as comprehension, beneath knowledge which takes itself to be indubitable of itself by itself. "If, in a first movement, Descartes takes a consciousness to be indubitable of itself by itself, in a second movement—the reflection on reflection—he recognizes conditions for this certitude" (TeI 186/TaI 210). In a second movement—that is, the critical reflection on the reflection characteristic of comprehension—Descartes recognizes conditions for the certitude of comprehension. This certitude, Levinas provisionally states, is due to the clarity and distinctness of the *cogito*. Levinas goes on to point out that while certitude is indeed due to the clarity and distinctness of the *cogito*, certitude itself is sought because of "the presence of infinity in this finite thought, which without this presence would be ignorant of its own finitude" (TeI 186/TaI 210). That is, without this presence, consciousness would be unable to posit and conceive its own finitude, its own doubt (TeI 185/TaI 210). It would be unable to be certain of its own doubt, unable to actualize the first movement. Levinas is referring here to the following famous passage from the Third Meditation in which Descartes counters his own query that perhaps his perception of the infinite is arrived at by negating the finite.

> On the contrary, I clearly understand that there is more reality in an infinite substance than in a finite one, and hence that my perception of the infinite, that is God, is in some way prior to my perception of the finite, that is myself. For how could I understand that I doubted or desired—that is, lacked something—and that I was not wholly perfect, unless there were in me some idea of a more perfect being which enabled me to recognize my own defects by comparison? (MPP 45–46/MFP 31)

How could Descartes understand that he doubted, how could he have posited and conceived his doubt, his finitude, his imperfection—which, in the Second Meditation, established the certitude of the *cogito* (that is, he understood, he was certain, he had no doubt, that he doubted)—unless there were always already in him some idea of a more perfect being which enabled him to recognize his own defects by comparison? Descartes here discovers in a second movement—that is, after the fact or in the critical reflection on the reflection characteristic of comprehension—the condition of the certitude characteristic

of the first movement, the condition of what was initially taken to be "indubitable of itself by itself," an absolute origin. Descartes discovers in the Third
Meditation a pre-originary origin—the infinite.

The *way* in which the infinite is articulated in the finite devolves from
the two distinct movements outlined earlier. Levinas establishes the proximity of this reading of Descartes' *Meditations* with his own descriptions of
death and the future, in that part of *Totality and Infinity* titled "Atheism or the
Will." The reading undertaken in this section, like the reading cited earlier,
characterizes the *Meditations* in terms of two distinct movements. The first
movement is called the chronological order and the second movement is
called the "logical" order. These two distinct movements are likewise articulated by the distinction between comprehension and critique.

> The being infinitely surpassing its own idea in us—God in the Cartesian
> terminology—subtends the evidence of the *cogito*, according to the
> third *Meditation*. But the discovery of this metaphysical relation in the
> *cogito* constitutes chronologically only the second move of the philoso-
> pher. That there could be a chronological order distinct from the "logi-
> cal" order, that there could be several moments in the progression, that
> there is a progression—here is separation. For by virtue of time this
> being is not *yet* [*n'est pas encore*]—which does not make it the same as
> nothingness, but maintains it at a distance [*à distance*] from itself. It is
> not all at once [*n'est pas d'un seul coup*]. (TeI 24–25/TaI 54)

It is important to keep in mind that the passages describing the *cogito* as "not
yet" and "not all at once" are written from the perspective of a reader/writer
who has discovered the infinite in the Third Meditation. It is at this moment,
that is, the moment of the discovery of the metaphysical relation in the *cogito*, that Levinas describes the *cogito* as "not yet" and "not all at once." The
condition of the actualization of the *cogito* is yet to come (note: from the perspective of the chronological order, the cogito is *already* assumed to be an
actual entity, indubitable of itself by itself). However, this does not make the
cogito the same as nothingness, or, the same as potency. At the moment of the
discovery of the infinite, the *cogito* is maintained at a distance from itself in
the interval between being and nothingness, between act and potency. It is
maintained in the interval of the not yet (or, the not all at once). It is this interval—an interval that marks the production of a trace of separation or alterity—that, I would suggest, Levinas calls "dead time" (*le temps mort*). Even
God is not yet. Even God is still to come. Levinas writes: "Even its [i.e., the
cogito's] cause, older than itself, is still to come [*est encore à venir*]. The
cause of being is thought or known by its effect *as though* it were posterior to
its effect" (TeI 25/TaI 54). The *cause* of being (God) is thought or known by

its *effect* (the *cogito*) *as though* the cause were posterior to its effect. Dead time marks the moment in comprehension when comprehension finds itself at a distance from itself. An attentive reading of Descartes' *Meditations* demands the critique (and, at the same time, the recognition) of comprehension. At this moment of the discovery of the infinite, that is, at this moment of critique (if only for a moment), what is critiqued (that is, comprehension) retains all of its value *in* the very critique.

Referring to these passages, Levinas writes: "Thus already theoretical thought [. . .] articulates separation" (TeI 25/TaI 54). "Theoretical thought" here refers to both comprehension and critique, which articulate not merely the reflection, but the production of separation. For "[s]eparation," Levinas writes, "is not *reflected* [*reflétée*] in thought, but *produced* [*produite*] by it" (TeI 25/TaI 54, emphasis added). To appreciate this passage fully it will be necessary to clarify what Levinas means by the term *production*.

Levinas introduces the ambiguous term *production* in the preface to *Totality and Infinity*. It designates both the effectuation of being and its being brought to light, that is, its appearance or revelation (TeI XIV/TaI 26). This ambiguous term is crucial for a proper understanding of the following passage, which, as will become apparent later, is likewise crucial for a proper understanding of Levinas's reading of Descartes' *Meditations*. The alterity of the other is not merely reflected within the thought of an I. Perhaps alluding to his consideration of the Cartesian *cogito*, Levinas writes: "It is in order that alterity be produced [*se produise*] *in being* that a 'thought' is needed and that an I is needed" (TeI 10/TaI 39). This suggests that the *cogito* is needed in order that alterity be produced in being. Thought, insofar as it is comprehension coupled with critique, is the very break-up of comprehension and the production (not merely the reflection) of transcendence. "We know this relation," Levinas writes, "only in the measure that we effect [*effectuons*] it; this is what is distinctive about it. Alterity is possible only starting from *me*" (TeI 10/TaI 40). We know the relation, we can reflect upon it, only in the measure that we *effect* it (that is, bring it about). But what is known or reflected upon in this effectuation, what is revealed, is *not* the unambiguous appearance of something, as is usually the case in production (which ambiguously conveys *both* effectuation *and* being brought to light or appearing). For what is produced in *this* effectuation is not something that unambiguously appears, but rather what infinitely approaches (or withdraws from) revelation and merely leaves a trace of itself in an ambiguity. Therefore, what is known or reflected upon is an irreducible ambiguity—a trace of what infinitely approaches (or withdraws from) revelation.

It is now possible to appreciate properly what Levinas means when he writes: "Separation is not *reflected* in thought, but *produced* by it" (TeI 25/TaI 54, emphasis added). Separation is produced by thought in that one *effects* a progression through the two movements of the *Meditations*, in the measure that one *effects* a performance of a reading of the *Meditations*. But what is reflected upon in this effectuation is *not* the appearance of something, as is usually the case in production (which ambiguously conveys *both* effectuation *and* being brought to light or appearing). For what is produced in *this* effectuation is an inversion of order with respect to the chronological order and the "logical" order. What is produced in *this* effectuation is the double origin of the *cogito* and God. "The ambiguity of Descartes's first evidence, revealing the I and God in turn without merging them, revealing them as two distinct moments of evidence mutually founding one another, characterizes the very meaning of separation. The separation of the I is thus affirmed to be non-contingent, non-provisional. The distance between me and God, radical and necessary, is produced [*se produit*] in being itself" (TeI 19/TaI 48). To borrow a phrase from another context in *Totality and Infinity*, one could write that the constituted becomes within constitution the condition of the constituting (TeI 101/TaI 128). What is produced in *this* effectuation is not something that appears unambiguously, but rather an irreducible ambiguity. What is produced in *this* effectuation is not something that appears unambiguously, but rather what infinitely approaches (or withdraws from) revelation and merely leaves a trace of itself in this ambiguity. Therefore, what is reflected upon is an irreducible ambiguity—a trace of what infinitely approaches (or withdraws from) revelation.

One must be careful here not to hypostatize the infinite. The infinite is not anything that first exists and then reveals itself. It is nothing other than the exceeding of limits. The *infinition* of infinity is its very mode of being.

> The production [*production*] of the infinite entity is inseparable from the idea of infinity, for it is precisely in the disproportion between the idea of infinity and the infinity of which it is the idea that this exceeding of limits is produced [*se produit*]. The idea of infinity is the mode of being, the *infinition*, of infinity. Infinity does not first exist, and *then* reveal itself. Its infinition is produced [*se produit*] as revelation, as a positing of its idea in *me*. It is produced [*se produit*] in the improbable feat whereby a separated being fixed in its identity, the same, the I, nonetheless contains in itself what it can neither contain nor receive solely by virtue of its own identity. (TeI XIV–XV/TaI 26–27)

The production of infinity's mode of being, its *infinition*, is inseparable from the idea of infinity. The *infinition* of the infinite is produced in the performance of a reading that progresses through the *Meditations* to the discovery of the necessary, yet impossible, idea of infinity *in* the I. The idea of infinity names this performance. It names the irreducible ambiguity of the chronological order and the "logical" order. Among all of Descartes' ideas, the idea of God or the infinite is, according to the Third Meditation, exceptional. Descartes' investigation makes use of the scholastic distinction between formal reality and objective reality. The formal reality of an object is the intrinsic reality of the object. Objective reality refers only to ideas. The objective reality of an idea is the representational content of the idea. It is the object as it is represented in an idea. With the exception of the idea of the infinite, it is conceivable that there is enough formal reality in the I, in the thinking thing, to be the cause of the objective reality contained in every idea possessed by the I. "[T]he idea of infinity is exceptional in that its *ideatum* surpasses its idea, whereas for the things the total coincidence of their 'objective' and 'formal' realities is not precluded; we could conceivably have accounted for all the ideas, other than that of Infinity, by ourselves" (TeI 19/TaI 49). The relation with infinity cannot be stated in terms of experience, because the *ideatum* of the idea of infinity surpasses its idea, because "infinity overflows the thought that thinks it." In fact, "[i]ts very *infinition* is produced [*se produit*] precisely in this overflowing" (TeI XIII/TaI 25). What is experienced is the effect of the overflowing, the effect of the performance of the two movements that produces an irreducibly ambiguous double origin. Yet all that the infinite is is its effect. All the infinite is is the revelation after the fact of the pre-originary origin (which is produced in the performance of the two movements that produces an irreducibly ambiguous double origin).

The effectuation of this double origin makes possible those descriptions of the *cogito* pointed out earlier—those descriptions which must have been written from the perspective of a reader/writer who has *already* effected a progression through the two movements of the *Meditations*. For example: the *cogito* is not yet, is not all at once, or God is still to come. Another example pointed out earlier: "The cause of being is thought or known by its effect *as though* it were posterior to its effect." The effectuation of an inversion of order, of a double origin, makes possible the production of this logically absurd inversion of the "posteriority of the anterior" (TeI 25/TaI 54) by thought. "Thus already theoretical thought," on the basis of the effectuation of an inversion of order, "articulates separation" (TeI 25/TaI 54). Returning to the sentence in question: "Separation is not reflected in thought, but produced by it. For in it," Levinas writes, reiterating the logically absurd inversion of the "posteriority of the anterior," "the *After* or the *Effect* conditions the *Before* or the *Cause*: the Before *appears* and is only welcomed" (TeI 25/TaI 54). It appears, however, only as the irreducible ambiguity of the chronological and "logical" orders. Therefore, what is reflected upon in this effectuation is *not* the unambiguous appearance of something, as is usually the case in production, but the ambiguous trace of what infinitely approaches (or withdraws from) revelation, of what is not yet.

The performance of the two movements of Descartes' *Meditations* is a production of a trace of the not yet of the *cogito* and the not yet of the infinite. The performance of these two movements is the production of a trace of the *cogito* as interrupted and the infinite as interrupting. It is the production of a trace of what Levinas calls "dead time."

The productionlessness characteristic of Levinas's reading of Descartes' *Meditations* is marked by dead time. Dead time marks the interval of the not yet. This interval of the not yet is a third notion between being and nothingness, between act and potency. "Its originality consists in being between two times," that is, I would suggest, between the time of the chronological order and the time of the "logical" order. "The rupture of historical and totalized duration [i.e., the chronological order], which dead time [*le temps mort*] marks, is the very rupture that creation operates in being" (TeI 29/TaI 58).[3] Recall that "creation" names one aspect evinced or described by the two irreducible movements of comprehension and critique; that is, it names one aspect of a "created freedom" (TeI 54/TaI 83). Dead time marks the relation without relation (*relation sans relation* or *rapport sans rapport*) (TeI 52, 271/TaI 80, 295) of the *cogito* and the infinite. The phrase *relation without relation* articulates the fact that one term of the relation—the infinite—absolves itself from the relation, infinitely approaches (or withdraws from) the relation, or said otherwise, merely leaves a trace of itself in the production of a double origin in which it, momentarily appearing as an origin, is interminably vulnerable to being reappropriated by the *cogito*.

It is important to note that, given this reading of Descartes' *Meditations*, there is not a simple step beyond totality described in Levinas's work. It is not as though the title of the work *Totality and Infinity* is a reflection of the judgement that one is called to step beyond totality to infinity. In the preface to *Totality and Infinity* Levinas writes that the "beyond" the totality and objective experience is "reflected *within* the totality and history, *within* experience" (TeI XI/TaI 23). It is as though the key word in the title *Totality and Infinity* is not, as many readers of Levinas would suggest, *infinity*, but *and*. That the production of separation is not beyond the totality and history is suggested in several passages throughout *Totality and Infinity*. For example, in a passage already quoted, Levinas writes: "The distance between me and God, radical and necessary, *is produced* [*se produit*] in being itself" (TeI 19/TaI 48, emphasis added). The infinite leaves a trace of itself *in* the production of an irreducibly ambiguous double origin.

Levinas returns to an extended reading of Descartes' *Meditations* in "God and Philosophy." In this essay his consideration of the two movements (or here, moments) of the *Meditations* makes explicit the interruption characteristic of the moment of the discovery of the infinite. Here one again sees the double origin of the *cogito* and the infinite: the unincludable infinite bears in a second movement of consciousness what in a first movement claimed to bear it.

> The actuality of the *cogito* is [. . .] interrupted by the unincludable, not thought but undergone in the form of the idea of the Infinite, bearing in a second moment of consciousness what in a first moment claimed to bear it. After the certainty of the cogito, present to itself in the second Meditation, after the "halt" which the last lines of this Meditation mark, the third Meditation announces that "in some way I have in me the notion of the infinite earlier than the finite—to wit, the notion of God before that of myself."[4] The idea of the Infinite, *Infinity in me*, can only be a passivity of consciousness. Is it still consciousness? There is here a passivity which cannot be likened to receptivity. Receptivity is a collecting that takes place in a welcome, an assuming that takes place under the force of the blow received. The breakup of the actuality of thought in the "idea of God" is a passivity more passive still than any passivity, like the passivity of a trauma through which the idea of God would have been put into us. (DP 106/GP 160–61)

The infinite is *in* me insofar as it *interrupts* a "me" that would comprehend or include it (that is, have it *in* me). That is, in some way I have received an idea, I have it in me, before there is an I that is capable of receiving it. That the infinite is necessarily yet impossibly in the finite is reflected in the prefix *in-* of the word *infinite*. In "God and Philosophy," Levinas writes: "[I]t is [. . .] as though—without wanting to play on words—the *in* of the Infinite were to signify both the *non* and the *within*" (DP 106/GP 160). This prefix signifies negation in the sense of "breaking-up"[5] and inclusion in the sense of immanence (or more provocatively, incarnation). "The idea of God is God *in* me, but God already *breaking up* the consciousness which aims at ideas" (DP 105/GP 160, emphasis added). It is necessarily in the finite insofar as it is the condition of the certitude of the *cogito*. "For," as Descartes writes, "how could I understand that I doubted or desired—that is, lacked something—and that I was not wholly perfect, unless there were *in* me some idea of a more perfect being which enabled me to recognize my own defects by comparison?" (MPP 45–46/MFP 31, emphasis added). That the necessary inclusion of the infinite in the finite is different from what is structured as a comprehension of a *cogitatum* by a *cogitatio* is due to the impossible inclusion of the infinite in the finite. The infinite is unincludable. It is impossibly in the finite insofar as it overflows the thought that would comprehend it, insofar as it is an in-comprehensible exteriority that is the uncondition of the certitude of the *cogito*. The in-comprehensible interrupts the comprehension characteristic of the first movement. "And yet," Levinas writes, "there is an idea of God, or God is in us, as though the being-not-includable were also an ex-ceptional relationship with me, as though the difference between the Infinite and what ought to include and comprehend it were a non-indifference of the Infinite to this impossible inclusion, a non-indifference of the Infinite to thought" (DP 105/GP 160). This non-indifference to the finite "amounts to a *cogitatio not comprehending* the *cogitatum* which affects it utterly. The Infinite affects thought by devastating it and at the same time calls upon it; in a 'putting it back in its place' it puts thought in place. It awakens it" (DP 109/GP 162).

Levinas's reading of the moment of the discovery of the infinite in the Third Meditation of Descartes' *Meditations* "works" its way—either explicitly or implicitly—into most of Levinas's works since its introduction in "Philosophy and the Idea of Infinity." This is not true, however, of Levinas's reading of another moment in Descartes' *Meditations*. Levinas's reading of the role of the evil genius in the *Meditations* is limited (as far as I know) to *Totality and Infinity*, where it is still further limited to the first few pages of that part titled "Truth Presupposes Justice." This part follows "The Investiture of Freedom, or Critique," which is an extended reading of the discovery of the infinite in the Third Meditation. The relation without relation of the *cogito* and the evil genius, like the relation without relation of the *cogito* and the infinite, is marked by dead time.

In that part of *Totality and Infinity* titled "Truth Presupposes Justice," Levinas points out that taking the *cogito* as the "first certitude"—which is characteristic of the first movement—constitutes "an arbitrary halt which is not justified of itself" (TeI 65/TaI 92–93). After the pathway of doubt taken in the First Meditation, which seems to leave everything doubtful, Descartes concludes at the beginning of the Second Meditation that the exercise of doubt itself is beyond doubt. He may doubt, for example, the reliability of his senses, but he has no doubt that he doubts. But taking the *cogito* as the first certitude constitutes, according to Levinas, an arbitrary halt that is not justified of itself since it can likewise be cast into doubt.

> Doubt with regard to objects implies the evidence of the exercise of doubt itself. To deny this exercise would be again to affirm this exercise. In the *cogito* the thinking subject which denies its evidences ends up at the evidence of this work of negation, although in fact at a different level from that at which it had denied. But it ends up at the affirmation of an evidence that is not a final or initial affirmation, for it can be cast into doubt in its turn. The truth of the second negation, then, is affirmed at a still deeper level—but, once again, one not impervious to negation. This is not purely and simply a Sisyphean labor, since the dis-

tance traversed each time is not the same; it is a movement of descent toward an ever more profound abyss which we elsewhere have called *there is* [*il y a*], beyond affirmation and negation. (TeI 65–66/TaI 93)

Here one sees Levinas take Descartes' argument to its logical extreme. Here Levinas takes Descartes down a path that Descartes started to journey, but, with no apparent justification, discontinued. Levinas outlines here, I would suggest, two movements not wholly unlike those outlined with respect to the *cogito* and the infinite. In both cases, dead time marks the moment when the *cogito* finds itself at a distance from itself. In this particular case, it is as if the certitude of the *cogito*—which is characteristic of the first movement—were not yet, as if every attempt to actualize it were interrupted in the very attempt. At this moment, if only for a moment, what is doubted retains all of its value in the very negation. Dead time, therefore, marks the alternation between doubt and refutation of doubt that is a spiraling movement of descent toward the *il y a*.

Levinas prefaces this part of *Totality and Infinity* by drawing an analogy between the spontaneous freedom of the I characteristic of the first movement and the fate of Gyges who not only sees without being seen, but also knows that he is not seen. "But does not Gyges's position involve the impunity of a being alone in the world, that is, a being for whom the world is a spectacle? And is not this the very condition for solitary, and hence uncontested and unpunished, freedom, and for certitude?" (TeI 62/TaI 90). Levinas calls this pure spectacle a "silent world," presumably because the spontaneous freedom and certitude of the I are uncontested by any revelation. Nothing exterior to the solitary I disturbs its silent interiority. But Gyges's position, that is, the first movement of Levinas's reading of Descartes' *Meditations*, is not as unequivocal as these remarks lead one to think. The spontaneous freedom and certitude of the I is always already haunted by the doubt arising from the evil genius, a disturbance that is seemingly distinct from the infinite's interruption of the *cogito* in the Third Meditation.

Levinas joins his own account of the *il y a*, the there is, that he had offered in *Existence and Existents* and in *Time and the Other*, with Descartes' description of the evil genius in the *Meditations*. The evil genius is introduced by Descartes to help him persevere in the suspension of his ordinary beliefs by reiterating his previous arguments in a more vivid form. The potency of the doubt arising form the evil genius arises from the possibility, not the actuality, of the evil genius, from the nagging possibility that things "which all seem to manifest themselves for good" only *seem* to manifest themselves for good. "The evil genius does not manifest himself to *state* his lie; he remains, as possible, behind things which all seem to manifest themselves for good. The possibility of their fall to the state of images or veils codetermines their apparition as a pure spectacle, and betrays the recess that harbors the evil genius; whence the possibility of universal doubt, which is not a personal adventure that happened to Descartes" (TeI 63/TaI 90). I would suggest that universal doubt is not a personal adventure that happened to Descartes because of what Levinas calls the "arbitrary halt" at the first change of level in the spiraling movement of descent toward the ever more profound abyss called the *il y a*. The equivocation characteristic of the spiraling movement of descent is a deepening on Levinas's part of the doubt arising from the evil genius as it is presented in Descartes' *Meditations*. It is a deepening of that equivocation that opens "that interspace between the illusory and the serious in which a subject who doubts breathes" (TeI 64/TaI 91).

This interspace is marked by the interval of dead time, which is *between* being and nothingness. The equivocal appearance, "which is not a nothing, is not a being either—not even an interior being, for it is nowise *in itself*" (TeI 63/TaI 91). The equivocal appearance of the phenomena is neither pure nothingness nor a straightforward appearance *in itself* which, as such, would enable one to dismiss it with certitude. Appearance is terrifying precisely because of this equivocality, precisely because it *might* deceive one.

This equivocal interspace likewise has consequences for the thinking subject. This is especially evident in that spiraling movement of descent that deepens the doubt arising from the evil genius as it is presented in the *Meditations*. The I in this spiraling movement of descent, in this "work of infinite negation" (TeI 66/TaI 93), does not find in the *cogito* itself a stopping place. Like the subject interrupted by the infinite, it dwells in the equivocal interval between being and nothingness. In this equivocal interspace in which there is neither *this* nor *that*, but there is simply *there is* (*il y a*) without one being able to fix a substantive to this term, the I is itself depersonalized. In that part of *Existence and Existents* titled "Existence without Existents" Levinas writes:

> The disappearance of all things and of the I leaves what cannot disappear, the sheer fact of being in which *one* participates, whether one wants to or not, without having taken the initiative, anonymously. Being remains, like a field of forces, like a heavy atmosphere belonging to no one, universal, returning in the midst of the negation which put it aside, and in all the powers to which that negation may be multiplied. (DEE 95/EE 58)

Like the subject interrupted by the infinite, the subject subjected to the spiraling movement of descent toward the *il y a* dwells in the equivocal interval between being and nothingness. This spiraling movement of descent that is the alternation between doubt and refutation of doubt outlines, I have already suggested, two movements not wholly unlike those outlined with respect to the *cogito* and the infinite. Even though Levinas prefaces this section of *Totality and Infinity* by positing an absolutely silent world that is "the very condition for solitary, and hence uncontested and unpunished, freedom, and for certitude" (TeI 62/TaI 90), his subsequent description calls this unequivocal world characteristic of the first movement into question. This world is fraught with equivocation. It is *not* simply silent ("[i]t is as though in this silent and indecisive apparition a lie were perpetuated, as though the danger of error arose from an imposture, as though the silence were but the modality of an utterance"), it is *not* simply solitary (it "comes to us from the Other, be he an evil genius"), it is *not* simply certain ("[t]he evil genius' lie [. . .] is in that interspace between the illusory and the serious in which a subject who doubts breathes"), and, as such, it is *not* uncontested (TeI 64/TaI 91). The first movement is interrupted by a second movement. The spontaneous freedom and certitude of the I is always already haunted by the doubt arising from the evil genius, a disturbance that is *seemingly* distinct from the infinite's interruption of the *cogito* in the Third Meditation.

This reading of Levinas's reading of Descartes' *Meditations* is disruptive on several different levels. First, doubling the two irreducible movements interrupts any linear reading of the *Meditations* that would easily step from the evil genius to the certitude of the *cogito*, and then to the *cogito*'s relationship with the infinite. That is, it interrupts any reading that would leave the evil genius behind, that would treat it as merely a step on the way to the *cogito*'s relationship with the infinite. Second, doubling the two irreducible movements likewise interrupts any linear reading of Levinas's work. One can locate such an interruption in the relationship of silence and language considered by Levinas in the context of his reading of Descartes' *Meditations*. Levinas writes that language is "an attitude of the same with regard to the Other irreducible to the representation of the Other, irreducible to an intention of thought, irreducible to a consciousness of . . . , since relating to what no consciousness can contain, relating to the infinity of the Other. Language is not enacted within a consciousness; it comes to me from the Other and reverberates in consciousness by putting it in question" (TeI 179/TaI 204). Language, for Levinas, is itself the relation without relation of the I and the infinity of the other. But the "total frankness ever renewed [*franchise totale, toujours renouvelée*]" (TeI 71/TaI 98) characteristic of language cannot simply be *opposed* (as Levinas sometimes leads one to think) to the "ever renewed equivocation [*équivoque toujours renouvelée*]" (TeI 63/TaI 91) characteristic of the doubt arising from the silence of the evil genius/*il y a*. By the same token, this silence cannot easily be inscribed in a linear reading that would situate it as a step on the way to the frankness of language. The "ever renewed frankness" is always already accompanied (haunted?) by the "ever renewed equivocation." In fact, the ever renewed equivocation is the "inverse of language" (TeI 64/TaI 91), the inverse of the ever renewed frankness characteristic of language. Rather than being opposed to one another, they seem to describe inverse sides of the same relationship. This calls any simple step from the equivocation arising from the evil genius/*il y a* into the frankness of language, into the frankness of the ethical relation with the other, into question. A clear and distinct distinction between the other and the *il y a* will be called incessantly into question throughout the book.

Chapter 2

Skepticism and the Blinking Light of Revelation

*[T]he question mark in this said [the enigma
of a God speaking in man and of man not
counting on any god], which, contrary to the
univocal logos of the theologians, is alternating, is the very pivot of revelation, of its blinking light.*
                    —*Levinas,* Otherwise than
                    Being or Beyond Essence

*An alternation which, admittedly, testifies to
the hesitation of our little faith.*
                    —*Levinas,* Beyond the Verse

Levinas's work incessantly frustrates attempts to reveal unequivocally
what is said. This is especially true with Levinas's work on God. The arrival of
revelation is interrupted. The light that otherwise would be a clear guide is
equivocal. The light of revelation is not a steady beacon but a blinking light.
The image of a lighthouse would be appropriate if one was not led to think that
the source of the blinking light *is* something that *then* announces itself in either
a univocal or an equivocal manner. As if, for example, God is something that
then reveals itself, either by means of a steady or a blinking light. For Levinas,
God is only as the interruption of order. This is especially evident when one
reads Levinas's work on God alongside his work on skepticism.

Readers of Levinas must remain attentive to the way his work incessantly calls itself into question. In the preface to *Totality and Infinity*, Levinas
writes:

The word by way of preface [*préface*] which seeks to break through the
screen stretched between the author and the reader by the book itself

[. . .] belongs to the very essence of language, which consists in continually undoing its phrase by the foreword [*l'avant-propos*] or the exegesis, in unsaying the said, in attempting to restate without ceremonies what has already been ill understood in the inevitable ceremonial in which the said delights. (TeI XVIII/TaI 30)

This prefatory word (or foreword) serves as an inaugural reminder that a reading of what is said in the book must always already be accompanied by an unsaying. It announces that the language of *Totality and Infinity* is not exempt from this responsibility of unsaying what is said. *Totality and Infinity* is a book that, by way of this prefatory word, interrupts itself. It calls what is said into question.

Thirteen years later in *Otherwise than Being* this prefatory word is not only formally thematized but, at the same time, written into the very argument and exposition of the text. This was almost certainly in response to readers such as Blanchot and Derrida who point out numerous ways *Totality and Infinity* can too easily be read. This response is called for because in most cases the once only prefatory word has to do all the work of unsaying what is merely said in *Totality and Infinity*. However, one notable exception is Levinas's reading of Descartes' *Meditations on First Philosophy*. Here there is an intratextual performance of what is merely announced extratextually by the prefatory word. Here there is the production of a work (Descartes', as well as Levinas's) that calls itself into question. In fact, the reading of Descartes' *Meditations* produced by Levinas in *Totality and Infinity* is, perhaps, not merely an anticipation of what he will later write into the very production of *Otherwise than Being*, but moreover, that which teaches him the way to produce a work that calls itself into question. For this reading—which plays both a decisive and a pervasive role in *Totality and Infinity*—is heavily drawn upon in Levinas' reading of skepticism and the saying of the otherwise than being in *Otherwise than Being*.

The profundity of the *Meditations* lies, for Levinas, in "[t]he ambiguity of Descartes's first evidence, revealing the I and God in turn without merging them, revealing them as two distinct moments of evidence mutually founding one another" (TeI 19/TaI 48). This ambiguous double origin of the *cogito* and the infinite is performed in a reading that progresses from the First Meditation to the discovery of the infinite in the Third Meditation. In the performance of this reading one discovers, "*after the fact*" (*après coup*; TeI 25/TaI 54) or in reflection (TeI 186/TaI 210), the condition of the cogito; that is, one discovers the condition of what was initially taken to be indubitable of itself by itself, an absolute origin. One discovers in the Third Meditation a pre-originary origin—the infinite. This performance is the production of a trace of the *infinition* of the infinite, of the infinite as interrupting the thought that thinks it.

For Levinas, Descartes' *Meditations* is characterized by "two times" (TeI 29/TaI 58) or "movements" (TeI 186/TaI 210): the chronological order (in which the *cogito* is the cause of the idea of the infinite) and the "logical" order (in which the infinite is the cause of the *cogito*). The comprehension characteristic of the chronological order is called into question by the critique characteristic of the "logical" order. In an attentive reading of Descartes' *Meditations* the movement of comprehension is necessarily transgressed by the movement of critique. However, the movement of comprehension must retain all of its value in the very transgression. An attentive reading of Descartes' *Meditations* demands the sacrifice (and, at the same time, the recognition) of comprehension, if only for an instant.

> That there could be a chronological order distinct from the "logical" order, that there could be several moments in the progression, that there is a progression—here is separation. For by virtue of time this being is not *yet*—which does not make it the same as nothingness, but maintains it at a distance from itself. It is not all at once. Even its [i.e., the *cogito*'s] cause, older than itself, is still to come. The cause of being is thought or known by its effect *as though* it were posterior to its effect. (TeI 25/TaI 54)

The *cogito* and God are maintained in the interval of the not yet (or the not all at once, or the still to come). It is this interval, I would suggest, that Levinas calls "dead time" (*le temps mort*). Referring to these passages, Levinas writes: "Thus already theoretical thought [. . .] articulates separation. Separation is not *reflected* in thought, but *produced* by it" (TeI 25/TaI 54, emphasis added). Separation is produced by thought in that one effects a progression through the two movements of the *Meditations*, in that one effects a performance of a reading of the *Meditations*. But what is reflected upon in this effectuation is not the unambiguous appearance of something, as is usually the case in production (which ambiguously conveys both effectuation of being and being brought to light or appearing; TeI XIV/TaI 26). For what is produced in this effectuation is an inversion of order with respect to the chronological order and the "logical" order. What is produced in this effectuation is the double origin of the *cogito* and God. What is produced in this effectuation is not something that unambiguously appears, but rather an irreducible ambiguity, a trace of what infinitely approaches (or withdraws from) revelation, of what is not yet. The performance of the two movements of Descartes' *Meditations* is a production of a trace of the not yet of the subject and the not yet of the infinite. The performance of these two movements is the production of a trace of the subject as interrupted and the infinite as interrupting. It is the production of a trace of what Levinas calls "dead time."

Here one sees a productionless production. Here one sees the unworking of the work of comprehension.

One also sees the unworking of the work of comprehension in Levinas's reading of the evil genius in Descartes' *Meditations*. Descartes concludes, in the wake of the pathway of doubt that seems to leave everything doubtful, that the exercise of doubt itself is beyond doubt; that is, he has no doubt that he doubts. But taking the *cogito* as the first certitude constitutes, according to Levinas, an arbitrary halt that is not justified of itself since it can likewise be cast into doubt. This alternation between doubt and refutation of doubt is the spiraling movement of descent toward the *il y a*. Levinas outlines here, I would suggest, two movements not wholly unlike those outlined with respect to the *cogito* and the infinite. In both cases, dead time marks the moment when the *cogito* finds itself at a distance from itself. In this particular case, it is as if the certitude of the *cogito*—which is characteristic of the first movement—were not yet, as if every attempt to realize it were interrupted in the very attempt. At this moment, if only for a moment, what is doubted retains all of its value in the very negation. Dead time, therefore, marks the alternation between doubt and refutation of doubt that is a spiraling movement of descent toward the *il y a*.

Levinas's reading of Descartes' *Meditations* in *Totality and Infinity* is, as was suggested earlier, an intratextual performance of what is merely announced extratextually by the prefatory word—the unsaying or calling into question of what is merely said. Here there is the production of a work (Descartes', as well as Levinas's) that calls itself into question. Early in *Otherwise than Being* Levinas addresses, in language nearly identical to his announcement of the prefatory word in *Totality and Infinity*, the methodological problem of saying the unsayable. "The *otherwise than being* is stated in a saying that must also be unsaid in order to thus extract the *otherwise than being* from the said in which it already comes to signify but a *being otherwise*" (AE 8/OB 7). The unsaying of the said is cast by Levinas in terms of conveying and betraying. As soon as the otherwise than being is conveyed, it is betrayed in the said that conveys it. "A methodological problem arises here, whether the pre-original element of saying (the anarchical, the non-original, as we designate it) can be led to betray itself by showing itself in a theme (if an an-archeology is possible), and whether this betrayal can be reduced; whether one can at the same time know and free the known of the marks which thematization leaves on it by subordinating it to ontology" (AE 8/OB 7). Playing on the ambiguity of the term *betray*, which designates both to mislead and to reveal, Levinas wonders whether in the inevitable betrayal of the saying conveyed in the said, the saying can be led to betray itself. He wonders whether the betrayal can be reduced, or said otherwise, whether the saying's betraying itself can be highlighted, freed from the marks of thematization. He wonders whether it can be clandestinely caught in the act or listened in upon, so to speak. It can, Levinas insists, if one is attentive to the ambiguous trace of "the pre-original element of saying" inscribed in the said, inscribed, for example, in Descartes' *Meditations.*

On the one hand, saying is the *way* the otherwise than being is said, the *way* the reduction of the betrayal is produced. But this is not the pre-original element of saying. It is, rather, that element of saying which is merely a particular form of the said, specifically, the way something (including the pre-original element of language) is said.

On the other hand, saying is the pre-original, an-archical, or excessive element of language that exceeds language. It is that which is otherwise than being. But as excessive it inevitably is betrayed in the said. However, it is as was noted in the previous paragraph, betrayed in a particular way. Saying, as the excessive element of language that exceeds language, leaves a trace of itself in an "ambiguous or enigmatic way of speaking" (AE 9/OB 7), "in the form of ambiguity, of diachronic expression" (AE 56/OB 44).

Saying on the one hand is the trace of saying on the other hand.

Saying "is produced [*se produit*] out of time or in two times without entering into either of them, as an endless critique, or skepticism, which in a spiralling movement makes possible the boldness of philosophy, destroying the conjunction into which its saying and its said continually enter" (AE 57/OB 44). This passage echoes the reading of Levinas's reading of Descartes' *Meditations* undertaken earlier—specifically, the production of two irreducible times, the chronological and the "logical" order (TeI 25/TaI 54) and the alternation between doubt and refutation of doubt that is a spiraling movement of descent (TeI 65–66/TaI 93)—as well as raises the question of the role of skepticism in the production of Levinas's work.

Skepticism is introduced in *Otherwise than Being* alongside Levinas's consideration of the saying and the said. Here the necessity of unsaying the said, of reducing the betrayal inevitably characteristic of the conveying of the otherwise than being, is likened to skepticism.

> Skepticism, at the dawn of philosophy, set forth and betrayed the diachrony of this very conveying and betraying. To conceive the *otherwise than being* requires, perhaps, as much audacity as skepticism shows, when it does not hesitate to affirm the impossibility of statement while venturing to *realize* this impossibility by the very statement of this impossibility. If, after the innumerable "irrefutable" refutations which logical thought sets against it, skepticism has the gall to return (and it always returns as philosophy's legitimate child), it is because in the contradiction which logic sees in it the "at the same time" of the contradictories is missing, because a secret diachrony commands this

ambiguous or enigmatic way of speaking, and because in general signification signifies beyond synchrony, beyond essence. (AE 9/OB 7, translation emended)

Skepticism ventures to realize the impossibility of statement by the very statement of this impossibility. The two—skepticism and refutation of skepticism—come together in the diachrony of the atemporal temporality of the instant, the moment when possibility turns into impossibility, when the two are endured without skepticism merely being compromised in the recognition of a contradiction. This "secret diachrony" of the atemporal temporality of the instant is not the synchrony of the "at the same time" of a contradiction (which would silence skepticism), but rather the not yet of dead time. Recall that in *Totality and Infinity*, dead time is marked not only by the alternation between doubt and refutation of doubt that is a spiraling movement of descent toward the *il y a* (TeI 65–66/TaI 93), but also by the alternation of the movement of comprehension and the movement of critique that is a trace of the infinite. The parallel between the couple skepticism and refutation of skepticism and the couple doubt and refutation of doubt is obvious enough. The parallel also can be extended to the couple *cogito* and infinite. Dead time marks, in Levinas's reading of the infinite in Descartes' *Meditations*, the moment in comprehension when comprehension finds itself at a distance from itself. This moment—in Levinas's reading of Descartes' *Meditations* and in his reading of skepticism—is the diachronic atemporal temporality of the instant in which comprehension, production, and possibility retain all of their value in their very critique. At the moment of critique, what is critiqued (comprehension, production, and possibility) retains all of its value and therefore returns. But the retention of its value is what skepticism and the infinite call into question; therefore skepticism and the infinite return. This alternation between skepticism and refutation of skepticism or between *cogito* and infinite signifies a temporality (AE 213/OB 167), it signifies the secret diachrony of the atemporal temporality of the instant, the moment when possibility turns into impossibility, the not yet of dead time, which can only leave a trace of itself in the alternation. Both alternations—of either the couple skepticism (doubt) and refutation of skepticism (refutation of doubt) or the couple *cogito* and infinite—are endured in this moment of diachrony.

But this parallel between skepticism and the saying of the otherwise than being does not relegate skepticism to being merely an aid to understanding the language of *Otherwise than Being*, and therefore something essentially external to the production of the work. On the contrary, the skeptical saying is bound ever more closely to the saying of the otherwise than being. It is as though the qualification *perhaps*, so prominent in skepticism's introduction at the beginning of the work, was increasingly obscured throughout the production of *Otherwise than Being* until finally, toward the end of the work, Levinas writes: "If the preoriginal reason of difference, non-indifference, responsibility, a fine risk, conserves its signification, the couple *skepticism* and *refutation of skepticism* has to make its appearance alongside of the reason in representation, knowing, and deduction, served by logic and synchronizing the successive" (AE 213/OB 167). Notice that the equivocal qualification *perhaps*, so prominent in skepticism's introduction at the beginning of the work, is here replaced by the unequivocal and emphatic phrase *has to*.

This passage on the couple skepticism and refutation of skepticism is located in that part of *Otherwise than Being* titled "Skepticism and Reason," which offers the most extensive treatment of skepticism in that work.

> The periodic return of skepticism and of its refutation signify a temporality in which the instants refuse memory which recuperates and represents. Skepticism, which traverses the rationality or logic of knowledge, is a refusal to synchronize the implicit affirmation contained in saying and the negation which this affirmation states in the said. The contradiction is visible to reflection, which refutes it, but skepticism is insensitive to the refutation, as though the affirmation and negation did not resound in the same time. Skepticism then contests the thesis that between the saying and the said the relationship that connects in synchrony a condition with the conditioned is repeated. (AE 213/OB 167–68)

The skeptical saying is inevitably refutable when there is a recognition—in a "second time" (AE 199/OB 156), that is, in reflection or after the event—of the condition of the skeptical saying; that is, a recognition of the *statement* of the impossibility of statement. But the skeptical saying does not merely allow itself to be walled up in the condition of its enunciation. It benefits from an ambiguity devolving from the very production of a contradiction that contests or negates it, that walls it up and domesticates it. It contests the thesis that the relationship between the two times integral to the production of a contradiction is merely a relationship of conditioned (the "first time") and condition (the "second time"), taken as though they both resounded in the same time.

> The truth of skepticism [i.e., the statement of "the rupture, failure, impotence or impossibility of discourse" (AE 214/OB 168)] is put on the same level as the truths whose interruption and failure its discourse states, as though the negation of the possibility of the true were ranked in the order restored by this negation, as though every difference were incontestably reabsorbed into the same order. But to contest the possibility of truth is precisely to contest this uniqueness of order and level. (AE 213–14/OB 168)

The production of the contradiction that contests the skeptical statement is compromised because it presupposes precisely what the skeptical statement calls into question—the uniqueness of order and level. The "at the same time" of the two times of the contradiction—which for traditional logic re-establishes the priority of the second time, the condition of the enunciation, by appropriating the first time into the second time—is precisely what the skeptical statement calls into question. With the compromise, skepticism returns, that is, the first time re-establishes its priority over the second time. However, this compromise is only momentary, since the skeptical statement is again vulnerable to refutation.

This perpetual alternation between the production of a contradiction and the compromise of a contradiction (which is the return of the signification contradicted) articulates the two inextricable moments of the production of a trace of saying. It articulates the production of a trace of that which has never been present, never appeared. "This trace does not belong to the assembling of essence. Philosophy underestimates the extent of the negation in this 'not appearing,' which exceeds the logical scope of negation and affirmation" (AE 214/OB 168). Philosophy underestimates the extent of the negation in this "*not* appearing" because the trace is neither merely the negation of appearance, the not appearing of that which exceeds language (as in the production of a contradiction that negates or refutes the skeptical saying) nor merely the appearing of that which exceeds language (as in the compromise of the contradiction). Each of these moments is merely one of two inextricable moments necessary for the production of a trace. It is a trace of a relationship with illeity that orders me to responsibility in an anarchic way. This relationship is "religion," which, Levinas adds, exceeds the psychology of faith and of the loss of faith (AE 214/OB 168).

Rather than its signification being merely refuted, reabsorbed, or consumed, that which exceeds language "conserves its signification" in the production of a trace. It "conserves its signification"—at least momentarily—in the production of a trace, in the perpetual alternation characteristic of "the couple *skepticism* and *refutation of skepticism*" (AE 213/OB 167).

This perpetual alternation or spiraling movement of the couple skepticism and refutation of skepticism echoes a passage on the saying of the otherwise than being that directly addresses the question of the revelation of God. That part of *Otherwise than Being* titled "From Saying to the Said, or the Wisdom of Desire" addresses the way the saying of the otherwise than being shows itself in the said. One particular paragraph of this section calls for close attention. It begins: "That the ontological form of the said could not alter the signification of the beyond being which shows itself in this said devolves from the very contestation of this signification" (AE 198/OB 156). That the conveying of the signification of the beyond being is not a complete betrayal of this signification, that the inevitable betrayal inherent in the conveying of the signification of the beyond being can be reduced, devolves from the very production of a contradiction that is the contestation of this signification. Following upon this provisional statement Levinas asks two provisional questions that will eventually call for a rereading: "How would the contestation of the pretension beyond being have meaning if this pretension were not heard? Is there a negation in which the sense of which the negation is a negation is not conserved?" (AE 198/OB 156). The significance of all three of these provisional sentences can be determined only within the context of a detailed explanation of the production of a contradiction, including of course the contradiction that is the contestation of the signification of the beyond being.

> The contradiction which the signification of the beyond being—which evidently is not—should compromise is inoperative without a second time, without *reflection* on the condition of the statement that states this signification. In this reflection, that is, only after the event [*après coup*], contradiction appears: it does not break out between two simultaneous statements, but between a statement and its conditions, as though they were in the same time. (AE 198–99/OB 156)

The signification of the beyond being should, according to Levinas, compromise the very contradiction that contests it. That this signification actually compromises the very contradiction that contests it devolves from the production of this contradiction. The production of a contradiction, which refutes the signification of the beyond being and reabsorbs it into the said, requires two times—the statement of the beyond being *and* the reflection on the condition of the statement that states this signification. Contradiction appears only in this reflection, that is, only after the event, when the two times are taken as though they were in the same time. The signification of the beyond being is, therefore, evidently not beyond being when, in reflection, it is discovered that the subject is the condition of the enunciation. The signification of the beyond being is betrayed. But, is there a betrayal, as the second provisional question asks, in which the sense of which the betrayal is a betrayal is not completely conserved? That is, can the betrayal be reduced?

This explanation of the production of a contradiction also raises the question of the proximity of the saying of the beyond being and the skeptical saying. The contradiction that is the contestation of the saying of the beyond being is, like the contradiction that is the contestation of the skeptical saying, produced in two times. The contradiction, which refutes the saying of the beyond being and the skeptical saying, is only visible to reflection which takes the two times as though they resounded in the same time.

But the saying of the beyond being, like the skeptical saying, does not allow itself to be walled up in the conditions of its enunciation. It likewise benefits from an ambiguity devolving from the very production of a contradiction that contests or negates it, that walls it up and domesticates it.

The way in which the saying of the beyond being does not allow itself to be walled up in the condition of its enunciation echoes one aspect of Levinas's reading of Descartes' *Meditations* in *Totality and Infinity*.

> The statement of the beyond being, of the name of God, does not allow itself to be walled up in the conditions of its enunciation. It benefits from an ambiguity or an enigma, which is not the effect of an inattention, a relaxation of thought, but of an extreme proximity of the neighbor, where the Infinite comes to pass. The Infinite does not enter into a theme like a being to be given in it, and thus belie its beyond being. Its transcendence, an exteriority, more exterior, more other than any exteriority of being, does not come to pass save through the subject that confesses or contests it. Here there is an inversion of order: the revelation is made by him that receives it, by the inspired subject whose inspiration, alterity in the same, is the subjectivity or psyche of the subject. (AE 199/OB 156)

The statement of the beyond being is inevitably refutable. The subject that merely confesses the infinite recognizes—in a second time, that is, in reflection or after the event—that *it* is the condition of the confession. It recognizes the statement of the beyond being as self-contradictory. Having recognized itself as the condition of the confession, it recognizes itself as the contestation of the confession. Said in the language of Levinas's reading of Descartes' *Meditations* in *Totality and Infinity*, the second time integral to the production of a contradiction, that is, the reflection on the condition of the first time (the pretentious statement or confession of the beyond being) is recognized as the chronological order in which the *cogito* is the cause of the idea of the infinite.

While the confession of the infinite by the subject inevitably contests the infinite, Levinas insists that the infinite does not come to pass, does not leave a trace of itself, save through the *subject* that confesses it or that contests it by recognizing itself as the condition of the enunciation. Or, said in the language of Levinas's reading of Descartes' *Meditations* in *Totality and Infinity*, the infinite does not come to pass, does not leave a trace of itself, save through the chronological order in which the *cogito* is the cause of the idea of the infinite. But this inevitable refutation or contestation is obviously only half of the story necessary for the infinite to come to pass, for the production of a trace of the infinite. Were it the whole story, the recognition of the contradiction would merely alter the signification of the beyond being, would merely domesticate the infinite by walling it up in the condition of its enunciation, thereby conceding that the last word belongs to logical, rational, philosophical discourse.

The other half of the story, devolving from the first half of the story, involves the infinite's resistance to being walled up in the condition of its enunciation. Levinas is perhaps a bit too unequivocal when he writes: the statement of the beyond being, of the name of God, does not allow itself to be walled up. Given the first half of the story, Levinas would perhaps be more accurate writing: the statement of the beyond being, of the name of God, does not merely allow itself to be walled up. It does not merely allow itself to be walled up in the condition of its enunciation because it benefits from an ambiguity with respect to the condition of the enunciation. That is, the condition of the enunciation is not, as it may appear on initial reflection, merely the subject. At a certain moment (the atemporal temporality of the instant) the subject recognizes—again, in a second time, that is, in reflection or after the event—that the condition of its confession is the infinite. Or, again said in the language of Levinas's reading of Descartes' *Meditations* in *Totality and Infinity*, there is the discovery of the "logical" order in which the infinite is the cause of the *cogito*. The second time integral to the production of a contradiction, that is, the reflection on the condition of the first time (the statement or confession of the beyond being) is recognized as the "logical" order rather than the chronological order. Here there is an inversion of order with respect to the condition of the enunciation. Paradoxically, the revelation is made by him or her that receives it. The confession or contestation of the infinite is made by him or her that is always already inspired by the infinite, by the inspired subject whose inspiration, alterity in the same, infinite within the finite, is the subjectivity or psyche of the subject.

The infinite can only come to pass, can only leave a trace of itself, in the irreducibly ambiguous double condition of its enunciation produced by Levinas's reading of Descartes' *Meditations*. This reading of Descartes' *Meditations* does not allow the two times integral to the production of a contradiction to be thought *merely* "as though they were in the same time" (AE 199/OB 156). This reading compromises the mere synchronization of the two times; it compromises the mere reabsorption of the first time (the statement or confession of the beyond being) into the second time (the recognition, after the event, of the condition of the enunciation) because it necessarily yet impossibly thinks the equiprimordiality of the chronological order (in which the *cogito* is the condition of the enunciation, that is, is the condition of the idea of the infinite) and the "logical" order (in which the infinite is the condition of the enunciation).

The logically absurd inversion of the condition of the enunciation of the beyond being does not, as Levinas writes in his reading of Descartes' *Meditations* in *Totality and Infinity*, "indicate an illusion" (TeI 25/TaI 54). It is not, as he writes in *Otherwise than Being*, "the effect of an inattention, a relaxation of thought, but of an extreme proximity of the neighbor, where the Infinite comes to pass" (AE 199/OB 156)—that is, it is the trace of the infinite, of the beyond being, of the otherwise than being.

The significance of the three provisional sentences that opened the paragraph in question can now be considered. The paragraph began: "That the ontological form of the said could not alter the signification of the beyond being which shows itself in this said devolves from the very contestation of this signification" (AE 198/OB 156). That the conveying of the signification of the beyond being is not a complete betrayal of this signification, that the inevitable betrayal inherent in conveying of the signification can be reduced, devolves from the very production of a contradiction that is the contestation of this signification. The two times integral to the production of a contradiction are prevented by Levinas's reading of Descartes' *Meditations* from merely being thought as though they were in the same time because the second time, which is integral to the production of a contradiction, is irreducibly ambiguous. There is, rather, a perpetual alternation between the *production of the contradiction* (when, according to the chronological order, the *cogito* is recognized as the condition of the enunciation of the signification of the beyond being) and the *compromise of the contradiction*, that is, the return of the signification of the beyond being (when, according to the "logical" order, the infinite is recognized as the condition of the enunciation). The infinite is inevitably refutable, contestable, contradictory—but it returns.

The second provisional sentence asks: "How would the contestation of the pretension beyond being have meaning if this pretension were not heard?" (AE 198/OB 156). The contradiction that is the contestation of the pretension beyond being could not be produced without two times, one of which is the statement or confession of the beyond being that is inevitably refutable but that returns as one moment of the perpetual alternation between the production of the contradiction and the compromise of the contradiction (which is the return of the signification contradicted). The pretension is heard (at least momentarily) because it is one moment of the perpetual alternation.

The third provisional sentence asks: "Is there a negation in which the sense of which the negation is a negation is not conserved?" (AE 198/OB 156). The answer: yes, when the two times integral to the production of a contradiction are prevented by Levinas's reading of Descartes' *Meditations* from merely being thought as though they were in the same time, when there is a perpetual alternation between the production of a contradiction and the compromise of the contradiction. The sense of which the negation is a negation is not conserved (at least not completely) because it is merely one moment of the perpetual alternation.

The second and third provisional sentences, presented in the form of questions, serve to articulate characteristics of the two inextricable moments of the production of a trace of the saying of the beyond being. This trace, as has already been pointed out, is produced by a necessary yet impossible reading, by a perpetual alternation between the production of a contradiction and the compromise of the contradiction (which is the return of the signification contradicted) neither of which can be extricated or abstracted from the other. With the trace, therefore, the signification of the beyond being, the pretension beyond being, is conserved. It is heard (at least momentarily) and, at the same time, the sense of which the negation is a negation is not conserved (at least not completely), because both "are" merely as moments of a perpetual alternation.

God, according to Levinas, is not revealed (or concealed) unambiguously. The phrase *relation without relation* is used by Levinas to articulate the fact that one term of the relation (that is, God) absolves itself from the relation, or said otherwise, merely leaves a trace of itself in the irreducibly ambiguous double origin of God and the subject that Levinas inextricably weaves in *Otherwise than Being* into the couple skepticism and refutation of skepticism. This weaving of the double origin of God and the subject and the couple skepticism and refutation of skepticism, weaves the two readings of Descartes' *Meditations* in *Totality and Infinity* (the reading of the infinite and the reading of the evil genius) ever more tightly. It is as though the two readings of Descartes' *Meditations* in *Totality and Infinity* become indistinguishable in *Otherwise than Being*. God merely leaves a trace of itself in the blinking light of a double origin and of an incessant alternation of the couple skepticism (doubt) and refutation of skepticism (refutation of doubt). Neither simply present nor simply absent, God infinitely approaches (or withdraws from) revelation. God "is" only as approach (or withdrawal). God is only as the interruption of the isolated subject, which for Levinas is the beginning of responsibility. Religion, for Levinas, is nothing but responsibility for the other. The relation without relation of the subject and God is an *à-Dieu*—an interminable approach of or going *to God* that is at the same time an interminable withdrawal or *good-bye*. The *à-Dieu* serves to gather together several movements. This "good-bye" of/to God has several different (are they different?) trajectories: good-bye of/to God as someone or something with which the subject is in an unambiguous relation insofar as God infinitely approaches (or withdraws from) revelation, and good-bye of/to God as transcendent guarantee of the Good insofar as God is indistinguishable from its own other, that is, the demonic, the *il y a*.

Chapter 3

The Body and the (Non)Sense in Sensibility

> *How the adversity of pain is ambiguous!*
> —*Levinas,* Otherwise than
> Being or Beyond Essence
>
> *Learn to think with pain.*
> —*Blanchot,* The Writing of the Disaster

Totality and Infinity calls for being read in a multiplicity of ways. Alphonso Lingis, the principle translator of Levinas's works into English, suggests that *Totality and Infinity* is "structured, classically, as a phenomenology in different strata, related as founding and founded" (AE/OB xv). Granted, the structure, and often the vocabulary, of *Totality and Infinity* lends itself to such a reading. But such a reading risks domesticating the interruptions of *Totality and Infinity*. It risks the possibility of *Totality and Infinity* being too easily read and appropriated by, for example, ethics or theology.

In chapter 2 I suggested that Levinas's reading of Descartes' *Meditations on First Philosophy* in *Totality and Infinity* is a notable exception to the lack of an intratextual production of what is announced extratextually by the prefatory word. I also suggested that this reading is perhaps not merely an anticipation of what Levinas will later write into the very production of *Otherwise than Being*, but moreover, that which teaches him the way to produce a work that calls itself into question. With this in mind it may perhaps be instructive to remain attentive to the way this reading plays both a decisive and a pervasive role, on innumerable levels, in the very structure of *Totality and Infinity*.

The reading of dead time is the hinge upon which turns Levinas's reading of Descartes' *Meditations*. The reading of dead time that was offered in chapters 1 and 2 requires, however, a deformalization or concretization. This is undertaken especially in sections 2 and 3 of *Totality and Infinity* where, I would suggest, dead time gets renamed at each successive stratum. The following passage from Derrida's "Violence and Metaphysics: An Essay on the Thought of Emmanuel Levinas" is, with certain qualifications, a characterization of the structure of *Totality and Infinity* consonant with this suggestion. "[I]n *Totality and Infinity* the thematic development is neither purely descriptive nor purely deductive. It proceeds with the infinite insistence of waves on a beach: return and repetition, always, of the same wave against the same shore, in which, however, as each return recapitulates itself, it also infinitely renews and enriches itself" (EeD 124n1/WaD 312n7). A reading of *Totality and Infinity* which begins with dead time will call into question a simple linear reading of sections 2 and 3 of *Totality and Infinity* and raise the question of the proximity of *Totality and Infinity* and *Otherwise than Being*. Dead time also names the site of a certain relationship of the infinite and the *il y a*.

———————

Readings of *Totality and Infinity* frequently focus on the first thirty-three pages (in the English translation) of section 3 ("Exteriority and the Face"), taking the face as their point of departure. I would suggest that one begin with the body which, as will become apparent in a moment, is not merely a site from which one can unproblematically begin anything. Specifically, I would suggest that one begin with the equivocality of the lived body and the physical body, appearing in its most primordial form (TeI 212/TaI 235) in the postponement of death in a mortal will, in the interval of the not yet or dead time.

This equivocation is first outlined in those two parts of *Totality and Infinity* titled "Representation and Constitution" and "Enjoyment and Nourishment." The equivocation outlined here will not merely be left behind but will be re-described throughout not only section 2, but also sections 3 and 4.

Levinas begins these two parts of section 2 by describing the movement proper to objectifying intentionality and by establishing the proximity of that movement to what he, in other contexts, calls the first movement of Descartes' *Meditations*. He begins, specifically, by directing the readers' attention to the privilege of representation that appeared with the first exposition of intentionality as a philosophical thesis. "The thesis that every intentionality is either a representation or founded on a representation dominates the *Logische Untersuchungen* and returns as an obsession in all of Husserl's subsequent work" (TeI 95/TaI 122). This pervasive domination of representation leads, Levinas contends, to transcendental philosophy.[1] Levinas contends that despite the fact that the object of representation (*noema*) is, according to Husserlian phenomenology, to be distinguished from the act of representation (*noesis*), that is, the giving of meaning (*Sinngebung*), the object of representation—insofar as it is reducible to *noemata* that remain correlative to the ani-

mating *noesis*, that is, reducible to the meaning or sense (*Sinn*) of the mean-
ing-giving (*Sinngebung*)—is a product of thought. Here Levinas establishes
the proximity of this negative movement of the Husserlian *epochē* characteristic of representation (TeI 98/TaI 125) to the first movement of Descartes'
Meditations. This reduction of the object of representation to *noemata* is, he
writes, "a question of what in Cartesian terminology becomes the clear and
distinct idea. In clarity an object which is first exterior *is given* that is, is delivered over to him who encounters it as though it had been entirely determined
by him. In clarity the exterior being presents itself as the work of the thought
that receives it" (TeI 96/TaI 123). Characterized by clarity, intelligibility is the
adequation of the thinker with what is thought. It is a mastery accomplished
as a giving of meaning, as the reduction of the object of representation to *noemata*. There is an essential correlation of intelligibility and representation (TeI
99/TaI 127). Descartes' clear and distinct idea, characterizing intelligibility,
manifests itself as entirely present and immanent to thought.

But this description of representation in Husserlian phenomenology is,
like the description of the first movement of Descartes' *Meditations*, "detached
from the conditions of its latent birth" (TeI 99/TaI 126). In Descartes' *Meditations* the certitude of consciousness—which is due to the clarity and distinctness of the *cogito*—is subtended by a second movement, by a "logical" order
distinct from the chronological order. The clarity and distinctness of the *cogito*
is subtended by the discovery of the infinite. With this discovery of a condition
for what was otherwise taken in a first movement as indubitable of itself by
itself, there is an inversion of order—the constituted becomes the condition of
the constituting—that produces an irreducibly enigmatic double origin, that
produces the separation (TeI 19/TaI 48), the relation without relation, of the I
and the infinite. This inversion of order that produces separation is likewise
operative in Levinas's description of representation and the elemental.

Representation, like the first movement of Descartes' *Meditations*, is "a
necessary moment of the event of separation" (TeI 95/TaI 122, emphasis
added), but it is merely one of two necessary moments. Representation, like
the first movement of Descartes' *Meditations*, is taken as an unconditioned
condition. Reiterating what he wrote in "Representation and Constitution,"
Levinas writes in "Enjoyment and Nourishment" that representation "consists
in the possibility of accounting for the object as though it were constituted by
a thought, as though it were a noema" (TeI 101/TaI 128). This possibility
reduces the represented to the unconditioned instant of thought. But in
"Enjoyment and Nourishment" Levinas makes it clear that the elemental sub-
tends this movement of representation. In the enjoyment of the elemental, "the
process of constitution which comes into play wherever there is representation is reversed. What I live from is not in my life as the represented is within
representation in the eternity of the same or in the unconditioned present of

cogitation" (TeI 101/TaI 128). If one persists in using the language of representational thinking, that is, if one insists on describing this "phenomenon" in terms of constitution, one runs up against an enigma. Notice how the following passage echoes Levinas's reading of Descartes' *Meditations* in which he describes the infinite as overflowing its meaning, as constituting what in a first movement claimed to constitute it.

> If one could still speak of constitution here we would have to say that the constituted, reduced to its meaning, here overflows its meaning, becomes within [*au sein de*] constitution the condition of the constituting, or, more exactly, the nourishment of the constituting. This overflowing of meaning can be fixed by the term alimentation. The surplus over meaning is not a meaning in its turn, simply thought as a condition—which would be to reduce the aliment to a correlate represented. The aliment conditions the very thought that would think it as a condition. (TeI 101/TaI 128)

That the constituted becomes *within* constitution the condition of the constituting is and remains, for representational thinking, enigmatic. The originality of the situation lies in the necessary yet impossible thinking of both representation as condition and the aliment as condition. It lies in the irreducible ambiguity of a double origin—of an ambiguity which is the trace of that which exceeds meaning, of a past that has never "traversed the *present* of representation" (TeI 103/TaI 130), of a future that is always yet to come.

Levinas situates this description of the production of separation within the context of the event of dwelling. The description of the event of dwelling in that part of *Totality and Infinity* titled "The Dwelling," like the description of separation outlined in "Representation and Constitution" and "Enjoyment and Nourishment," is informed by Levinas's reading of Descartes' *Meditations*. Recalling the description of an inversion of order in "Enjoyment and Nourishment," Levinas writes: "Representation is conditioned. Its transcendental pretension is constantly belied by the life that is already implanted in the being representation claims to constitute. But representation claims to substitute itself *after the event* [*après coup*] for this life in reality, so as to constitute this very reality" (TeI 143/TaI 169).[2] The transcendental pretension of representation is constantly subtended by the elemental. But representation, conditioned by the elemental, claims to constitute this reality. That this conditioning of representation by the elemental could be reversed after the fact (*après coup*) results from the very production of separation.

> That representation is conditioned by life, but that this conditioning could be reversed after the event [*après coup*]—that idealism is an eter-

nal temptation—results from the very event of separation, which must
not at any moment be interpreted as an abstract cleavage in space. The
fact of the after-the-event [*l'après-coup*] does show that the possibility
of constitutive representation does not restore to abstract eternity or to
the instant the privilege of measuring all things; it shows, on the contrary, that the production [*production*] of separation is bound to time,
and even that the articulation of separation in time is produced [*se produit*] thus in itself and not only secondarily, for us. (TeI 144/TaI 169)

It is important to note that the reversal or inversion of the order of the elemental and representation is operative in both directions, though Levinas
explicitly outlines only one direction in this passage: representation, conditioned by the elemental, can be reversed after the event; that is, representation
is the condition of the elemental. But it is likewise the case that representation, condition of the elemental, can be reversed after the event; that is, representation is conditioned by the elemental.[3] The fact of the after-the-event
does show, therefore, that constitutive representation is *merely* a possibility. It
is merely *one* possibility among the two possibilities of a double origin, since
it perpetually alternates with the elemental understood as a condition. As
merely one pole of a perpetually alternating double origin constitutive representation does not, therefore, "restore to abstract eternity or to the instant the
privilege of measuring all things" (TeI 144/TaI 169). This restoration is interrupted, perpetually. The fact of the after-the-event shows, moreover, that the
production of separation is bound to time, it is bound to the perpetual recognition, after the fact (*après coup*), of the condition of what in a first movement
is taken to be a condition. It is again important to note that the production or
performance of this inversion of order is operative, as was stated above, in
both directions, perpetually. That the production of separation is bound to
time recalls Levinas's reading of Descartes' *Meditations*. Drawing upon a passage in *Totality and Infinity* referring specifically to Levinas's reading of
Descartes' *Meditations*, but equally applicable to the relationship of the I of
representation and the elemental, one could write: The ambiguity of what conditions what, revealing the I of representation and the elemental in turn without merging them, revealing them as two distinct moments of evidence mutually founding one another, characterizes the very meaning of separation. The
separation of the I is thus affirmed to be non-contingent, non-provisional. The
distance between me and the elemental, radical and necessary, is produced in
being itself (see TeI 19/TaI 48). Even "the articulation of separation in time,"
Levinas continues, "is produced thus in itself and not only secondarily, for us"
(TeI 144/TaI 169). It is not as though separation existed before it was articulated in time. Separation in itself is produced only in the event of articulation,
only in the event of producing or performing an inversion of order.[4] What *is*

produced "secondarily, for us," that is, what can be reflected upon (TeI 10, 25/TaI 40, 54) or known (TeI 144/TaI 170), is an ambiguous double origin. What *is* produced "secondarily, for us" is *not* the unambiguous appearance of something (as is usually the case in the effectuation of production), but rather the equivocal trace of what withdraws from appearance—a separated being as not yet and an absolute exteriority as not yet. *This* production obviously calls into question the designation *in itself*, for separation can be something in itself only in being produced as an irreducibly ambiguous double origin, that is, only in *not* being something in itself.

The next paragraph of the text explicitly situates this description of the event of separation within the context of the event of dwelling.

> The possibility of a representation that is constitutive but already rests on the enjoyment of a real completely constituted indicates the radical character of the uprootedness of him who is recollected in a home, where the I, while steeped in the elements, takes up its position before a Nature. The elements in and from which I live are also that to which I am opposed. The feat of having limited a part of this world and having closed it off, having access to the elements I enjoy by way of the door and the window, realizes extraterritoriality and the sovereignty of thought, anterior to the world to which it is posterior. *Anterior posteriorly* [*Antérieure postérieurement*]: separation is not thus "known"; it is thus produced [*se produit*]. (TeI 144/TaI 169–70)

In the context of his reading of Descartes' *Meditations*, Levinas writes: "The cause of being [i.e., God] is thought or known by its effect *as though* it were posterior [*postérieure*] to its effect" (TeI 25/TaI 54). Levinas uses the paradoxical formula *the posteriority of the anterior* (*la postériorité de l'antérieur*) to describe this irreducible ambiguity. Levinas draws upon this reading when he writes that extraterritoriality and the sovereignty of representational thinking, the feat of being independent of the elemental, is "anterior to the world to which it is posterior." The effectuation of an incessant inversion of order that is the production of a double origin is dwelling. Dwelling is both the independence of representation and the dependence of being steeped in the elemental, neither merely the independence of representation nor the dependence of being steeped in the elemental. The productionless production of separation or dwelling is marked or named by dead time, the interval of the not yet. That is, the effectuation of the perpetual alternation characteristic of separation or dwelling articulates the not yet of independence and the not yet of dependence.

Dwelling or separation is a way of being articulated by the body. "A being has detached itself from the world from which it still nourishes itself!

[. . .] There is here an ambiguity of which the body is the very articulation"
(TeI 88–89/TaI 116). The body is the accomplishment or production of the
irreducibly ambiguous double origin of the independence of representation
and the dependence of being steeped in the elemental. "The body naked and
indigent identifies the *center* of the world it perceives, but, *conditioned* by its
own representation of the world, it is thereby as it were torn up from the center from which it proceeded, as water gushing forth from rock washes away
that rock" (TeI 100/TaI 127). The body is the effectuation of a perpetual inversion of order. The body is the very reverting of the subject that represents into
a living from.

> The body is a permanent contestation of the prerogative attributed to
> consciousness of "giving meaning" to each thing; it lives as this con-
> testation. The world I live in is not simply the counterpart or the con-
> temporary of thought and its constitutive freedom, but a conditioning
> and an antecedence. The world I constitute nourishes me and bathes me.
> It is aliment and "medium" [«*milieu*»]. The intentionality aiming at the
> exterior changes direction in the course of its very aim by becoming
> interior to the exteriority it constitutes, somehow comes from the point
> to which it goes, recognizing itself past in its future, lives from what it
> thinks. (TeI 102/TaI 129)

If one persists, as Levinas does here, in using the language of intentionality,
one runs up against an enigma. It is as though intentionality aiming at an exterior inverts direction *in the course* of its aim. This incessant inversion that is
the production of an irreducibly ambiguous double origin of representation
and the elemental formally parallels, I would suggest, Levinas's reading of
Descartes' *Meditations*.[5]
   That the body's concrete articulation of the production of separation or
dwelling formally parallels Levinas's reading of Descartes' *Meditations* is further substantiated in that part of *Totality and Infinity* titled "Labor, the Body,
Consciousness," where Levinas thematizes two aspects of the body. These two
aspects of the body—lived body and physical body—articulate two movements not formally unlike the two movements of Descartes' *Meditations*.

> Life is a body, not only lived body [*corps propre*], where its self-suffi-
> ciency emerges, but a cross-roads of physical forces, body-effect. In its
> deep-seated fear life attests this ever possible inversion of the body-
> master into body-slave, of health into sickness. *To be a body* is on the
> one hand *to stand* [*se tenir*], to be master of oneself, and, on the other
> hand, to stand on the earth [*se tenir sur terre*], to be in the *other*
> [*l'autre*], and thus to be encumbered by one's body. (TeI 138/TaI 164)[6]

Here Levinas seems to make a distinction between standing, detached from its concrete conditions (which articulates the independence of the I of representation), and "standing on the earth, in the other" (which articulates the dependence upon the elemental). This irreducible ambiguity of independence and dependence describes the production of separation or dwelling; it describes "the radical character of the uprootedness of him who is recollected in a home" (TeI 144/TaI 169). This irreducible ambiguity is articulated by the body, that is, by the lived body and the physical body.

> To be at home with oneself in something other than oneself, to be oneself while living from something other than oneself, to live from . . . , is concretized in corporeal existence. "Incarnate thought" is not initially produced [*se produit*] as a thought that acts on the world, but as a separated existence which affirms its independence in the happy dependence of need. It is not that this equivocation amounts to two successive points of view on separation; their simultaneity constitutes the body. To neither of the aspects which reveal themselves in turn does the last word belong. (TeI 139/TaI 164–65)

This passage not only re-articulates "the radical character of the uprootedness of him who is recollected in a home," it is also reminiscent of Levinas's description of the double origin of the *cogito* and the infinite in Descartes' *Meditations*. In the passage just cited Levinas writes the following about the two aspects of the body: "To neither of the aspects which reveal themselves in turn [*se révèlent tour à tour*] does the last word belong." This is remarkably similar in form and vocabulary to the following passage: "The ambiguity of Descartes's first evidence, revealing the I and God in turn [*révélant, tour à tour*] without merging them, revealing them as two distinct moments of evidence mutually founding one another, characterizes the very meaning of separation" (TeI 19/TaI 48). The two aspects of the body—lived body and physical body—articulate two movements not unlike the two movements of Descartes' *Meditations*.

This irreducible ambiguity of the body—which articulates the not yet of the lived body and the not yet of the physical body that is "a sector of an elemental reality" (TeI 140/TaI 165)—is, according to Levinas, consciousness. The description of consciousness as "disincarnation" in the following passage is similar to the description of dwelling as "uprootedness": "Consciousness does not fall into a body—is not incarnated; it is a disincarnation—or, more exactly, a postponing of the corporeity of the body" (TeI 140/TaI 165–66), the not yet of the physical body, the not yet of complete dependence upon the elemental. To describe conscious as postponement is—as is the case in Levinas's description of the *cogito* in Descartes' *Meditations* as not yet or not all at once—to describe it as always already in relation to the other. Consciousness, therefore, is produced in the effectuation of a double origin. It is produced concretely, in the event of dwelling or separation.

> To be conscious is to be in relation with *what is*, but as though the present of *what is* were not yet [*n'était pas encore*] entirely accomplished and only constituted the *future* of a recollected being. To be conscious is precisely to have time—not to exceed the present time in the project that anticipates the future, but to have a distance [*une distance*] with regard to the present itself, to be related to the element in which one is settled as to what is not yet [*n'est pas encore*] there. All the freedom of inhabitation depends on the time that, for the inhabitant, still always remains. (TeI 140/TaI 166)

Insofar as consciousness names that *moment in* the intentionality of the lived body when intentionality finds itself at a distance *from* itself, the term *consciousness* undergoes slippage.[7] It names the irreducibly ambiguous body as the "site" of a moment when a rigorous phenomenological description (at least as it is read by Levinas in *Totality and Infinity*) calls itself into question.

The irreducible ambiguity of the body articulates dead time. It articulates the interval of the not yet that marks the event of dwelling or separation. This interval, marking the relation without relation or double origin of the I of representation and the elemental *can* be characterized as enjoyment. "Sensibility establishes a relation with a pure quality without support, with the element. Sensibility is enjoyment. The sensitive being, the body, concretizes this *way of being*, which consists in finding a condition in what, in other respects, can appear as an object of thought, as simply constituted" (TeI 109/TaI 136). But the interval of the not yet, marking the ambiguous relationship of the I of representation and the elemental, can *at the same time* be characterized as menace and insecurity.

> —The distance with regard to the element to which the I is given over menaces [*menace*] it in its dwelling only in the future. (TeI 140/TaI 166)

> —The dwelling, overcoming the insecurity [*l'insécurité*] of life, is a perpetual postponement [*perpétuel ajournement*] of the expiration in which life risks foundering. The consciousness of death is the consciousness of the perpetual postponement [*l'ajournement perpétuel*] of death, in the essential ignorance of its date. Enjoyment as the body that labors maintains itself in this primary postponement [*dans cet ajournement premier*], that which opens the very dimension of time. (TeI 139/TaI 165)

This menace or insecurity maintains itself, like enjoyment, in the primary postponement of death, that is, in dead time, in the interval of the not yet. It is important to keep in mind, therefore, that the descriptions of the relation without relation or double origin operative in section 2 of *Totality and Infinity* address the relationship of the I of representation and the elemental, rather than the relationship of representation and enjoyment (as the text sometimes leads one to think), since enjoyment, I would suggest, is only one perspective on the relationship of representation and the elemental.

The perfidious elemental—which "gives itself while escaping," which "on the one hand offers itself and contents, but which already withdraws, losing itself in the *nowhere*"—"opens up an abyss within [*dans*] enjoyment itself" (TeI 115/TaI 141). Levinas joins this description of the elemental with his description of the *il y a* that he had himself offered in *Existence and Existents* and in *Time and the Other*. "What the side of the element that is turned toward me conceals is not a 'something' susceptible of being revealed, but an ever-new depth of absence, an existence without existent, the impersonal par excellence. [. . .] Enjoyment is without security. [. . .] [I]nsecurity menaces [*l'insécurité menace*] an enjoyment already happy in the element, rendered sensitive to disquietude only by this happiness" (TeI 116/TaI 142). The irreducibly ambiguous body articulates a relationship—marked by the interval of the not yet—of the I of representation and the elemental that can be characterized as either enjoyment or menace and insecurity. One must be careful not to read this ambiguous characterization in a linear manner, as if one enjoys the elemental and *then* one is menaced (or vice versa). The interval of the not yet marks at one and the same time enjoyment and menace. "Enjoyment is without security."

But this ambiguous characterization of the interval of the not yet is multiplied by the fact that this same interval—an interval that is articulated, as I suggested above, by the event of dwelling or separation—likewise marks the relationship of the I of representation and the other as infinite.

> But the transcendence of the face is not enacted outside of the world, as though the economy by which separation is produced [*se produit*] remained beneath a sort of beatific contemplation of the Other [*Autrui*] (which would thereby turn into the idolatry that brews in all contemplation). The "vision" of the face as face is a certain mode of [*une certaine façon de*] sojourning in a home, or—to speak in a less singular fashion—a certain form of [*une certaine forme de*] economic life. No human or interhuman relationship can be enacted outside of economy; no face can be approached with empty hands and closed home. Recollection in a home open to the Other [*Autrui*]—hospitality—is the concrete and initial fact of human recollection and separation; it coincides

[*coïncide*] with the Desire for the Other [*Autrui*] absolutely transcendent. The chosen home is the very opposite of a root. It indicates a disengagement, a wandering [*errance*] which has made it possible, which is not a *less* with respect to installation, but the surplus of the relationship with the Other [*Autrui*], metaphysics. (TeI 147/TaI 172)

Sojourning in a home, as was indicated earlier, is both the independence of representation and the dependence of being steeped in the elemental, neither merely one nor the other. Recollected in a home, one is steeped in the elemental. Here one sees nearly an identical structure. But here, recollected in a home, one is open not to the elemental, the other (*autre*), but to the other (*Autrui*). The transcendence of the face is "a certain mode" of dwelling. Dwelling "coincides" with the desire for the absolutely transcendent other (*Autrui*). Dwelling indicates a surplus which has made it possible, a surplus that has interrupted the independence of representation and that leaves a trace of itself in an irreducibly ambiguous double origin. The home is again the very opposite of a root. But here it indicates not the surplus of the relationship with the elemental, but the surplus of the relationship with the other (*Autrui*). This relationship of the I of representation and the other (*Autrui*) is characterized by Levinas as responsibility.

Here, as in several other places in *Totality and Infinity*, one can locate a certain interruption of the text—an interruption of a simple step beyond section 2 ("Interiority and Economy") into section 3 ("Exteriority and the Face"). It is worth pausing for a moment at the threshold of sections 2 and 3 of *Totality and Infinity* to anticipate the aporia of death to be considered in chapter 4 and its role in a characterization of enjoyment that blurs the rigid distinctions Levinas sometimes makes in *Totality and Infinity* among consciousness, sensibility as enjoyment, and the face of the other.

Enjoyment is read as self-sufficiency. It comes into play as a withdrawal into oneself, an involution or "coiling" movement of a spiral (TeI 91/TaI 118). In *Otherwise than Being* enjoyment is described as "the singularization of an ego in its coiling back upon itself" (AE 93/OB 73). It is this self-sufficiency that "suffices to itself in a world insufficient for thought" (TeI 109/TaI 135) that, according to some readings, is *then* interrupted by the other. First, *Totality and Infinity* betrays Levinas's explicit intention to disengage sensibility as enjoyment from thought. Enjoyment is, as I have already suggested, an articulation of both the independence of the I of representation and the dependence upon the elemental, neither merely one nor the other. Representation is a "necessary moment of the event of separation" (TeI 95/TaI 122), of the interval of the not yet marking the relation (called sensibility as enjoyment) of the I and the elemental. Second, the not yet of sensibility as enjoyment marks the self-sufficiency of the I, but "the image we have used of the spiral that coils over itself does not enable us to depict also the enrootedness of this sufficiency in the insufficiency of living from . . ." (TeI 116/TaI 143). The not yet of sensibility as enjoyment is (like death, as will become apparent in the following chapters) both singularizing and exposure. The not yet of sensibility as enjoyment (lived as the ambiguity of the body) that articulates the "for itself" of singularity, likewise articulates (or cannot be rigidly distinguished from) the exposure characteristic of the not yet. One can say that the not yet of sensibility as enjoyment is itself both singularizing and exposure. Or, one can say that the interval of the not yet—articulated by the irreducibly ambiguous body—articulates a relationship with the other that can be characterized as enjoyment, menace/insecurity, or responsibility, all of which are singularizing *and* exposure. Despite Levinas's attempts in *Totality and Infinity* to establish and maintain a rigid distinction, there is blurring.

The ambiguity of the other as *il y a* and the other as infinite—an ambiguity gathered around dead time and articulated by the irreducibly ambiguous body, the sensitive being—is reiterated in that part of section 3 of *Totality and Infinity* titled "The Ethical Relation and Time." In "The Ethical Relation and Time" the other—insofar as its relationship with the subject can be characterized as menace and insecurity—is, I would suggest, expanded in section 3 of *Totality and Infinity* to encompass not only the elemental (as is the case in section 2) but also the faceless other encountered in war and commerce. It is also important to note that in this part of *Totality and Infinity* the interval of the not yet, which marks the relationship of the subject and the other, is not only characterized as menace and insecurity (as well as enjoyment and responsibility), but also as violence. "Violence bears upon only a being both graspable and escaping every hold" (TeI 198/TaI 223). It is, as described above, the body that concretely articulates this ambiguity. Here—as in that part of section 2 titled "Labor, the Body, Consciousness"—Levinas describes the body in terms of a series of irreducible distinctions such as lived body/physical body, body-master/body-slave, and health/sickness. "The body exceeds the categories of a thing, but does not coincide with the role of 'lived body' [*«corps propre»*] which I dispose of in my voluntary action and by which *I can*" (TeI 205/TaI 229). The body exceeds the categories of a thing, but it is incessantly not yet merely the I of representation. Because the body is both not yet the lived body and not yet the physical body, it can be taken as merely a constituting I or as merely a thing.

> The body in its very activity, in its for itself [which refers to the lived body, the body-master, health], inverts into a thing to be treated as a thing [which refers to the physical body, the body-slave, sickness, i.e., to the body as "a sector of an elemental reality" (TeI 140/TaI 165), insofar as it is hypostatized by an other as a mere thing]. This is what we express concretely in saying that it abides between health and sickness. (TeI 205/TaI 229)

It is important to keep in mind, however, that even though the body *can* be taken as merely a thing (by the hypostatization of the other) or as merely a constituting I, "[o]ne does not adopt successively [*successivement*] and independently the biological point of view on it and the 'point of view' [«*point de vue*»] which from the interior maintains it as a lived body [*corps propre*]; the originality of the body consists of the coinciding of two points of view [*points de vue*]" (TeI 205/TaI 229). This passage echoes an earlier articulation of the irreducible ambiguity of the body—"It is not that this equivocation amounts to two successive points of view [*deux points de vue successifs*] on separation; their simultaneity constitutes the body. To neither of the aspects which reveal themselves in turn [*se révèlent tour à tour*] does the last word belong" (TeI 139/TaI 165)—that, at least in part, is remarkably similar in form and vocabulary to the following passage: "The ambiguity of Descartes's first evidence, revealing the I and God in turn [*révélant, tour à tour*] without merging them, revealing them as two distinct moments of evidence mutually founding one another, characterizes the very meaning of separation" (TeI 19/TaI 48). The irreducible ambiguity of the body "is the paradox and the essence of time itself proceeding unto death, where the will is affected as a thing by the things [. . .] but gives itself a reprieve and postpones the contact by the against-death of postponement. The will essentially violable harbors treason in its own essence" (TeI 205/TaI 229). The irreducible ambiguity of the body articulates dead time, the interval of the not yet. In the following passage, Levinas gathers together the three characterizations of the interval of the not yet (enjoyment, menace/insecurity/violence, and responsibility), while at the same time noting that they each can drift into the other:

> The corporeity of the will must be understood on the basis of this ambiguity of voluntary power, exposing itself to the others [*autres*] in [*dans*] its centripetal movement of egoism [which refers to enjoyment (see TeI 91, 116/TaI 118, 143)]. The body is its ontological regime, and not an object. The body, where expression can dawn forth and where the egoism of the will becomes discourse and primal opposition, at the same time [*en même temps*] conveys the entry of the I into the calculations of the Other [*autrui*]. (TeI 206/TaI 229–30)

Dead time—articulated by the irreducibly ambiguous body—is ambiguous. The body, as the site of the relationship with the other, is the site of enjoyment, exposure to menace/insecurity/violence, and responsibility. Or, said in the language of *Otherwise than Being*, the body is the site of enjoyment, the by-the-other (or non-sense), and the for-the-other (or sense). This irreducible ambiguity of the body is founded in mortality.

It is in mortality that the interaction of the psychic and the physical appears in its primordial form. The interaction of the physical and the psychic, when approached from the psychic, posited as for itself or as *causa sui*, and from the physical, posited as unfolding in function of the "other," gives rise to a problem due to the abstraction to which the terms in relation are reduced. Mortality is the concrete and primary phenomenon. It forbids the positing of a for itself that would not be already delivered over to the Other and consequently be a *thing*. The for itself, essentially mortal, does not only represent things to itself, but is subject to them. (TeI 212/TaI 235)

The equivocality of the lived body and the physical body, the psychic and the physical, appears in its most primordial form in the postponement of death in a mortal will, in the interval of the not yet or dead time.

Chapter 4

On the Genealogy of Death

> *Death threatens me from beyond. This unknown*
> *that frightens, the silence of the infinite spaces*
> *that terrify, comes from the other, and this alter-*
> *ity, precisely as absolute, strikes me in an evil*
> *design or in a judgment of justice.*
> *—Levinas,* Totality and Infinity

The formal analysis of dead time in Levinas's reading of Descartes' *Meditations* is to be read alongside Levinas's work on death. One of the defining elements (if not *the* defining element) of Levinas's work on death is the way in which it is situated with respect to Heidegger's work. Levinas rarely mentions death without mentioning the existential analysis of death in Heidegger's *Being and Time*. Levinas frequently reads death in *Being and Time* as *merely* possibility. In *Time and the Other* Levinas writes: "Being toward death, in Heidegger's authentic existence, is a supreme lucidity and hence a supreme virility. It is *Dasein's* assumption of the uttermost possibility of existence, which precisely makes possible all other possibilities, and consequently makes possible the very feat of grasping a possibility—that is, it makes possible activity and freedom" (TA 57/TO 70). Being toward death, in Heidegger's authentic existence, is, according to Levinas, a supreme virility, "the virility of grasping the possible, the *power to be able* [*pouvoir de pouvoir*]" (TA 73/TO 82). Or, said otherwise in a footnote to the passage cited at the beginning of this paragraph, "[d]eath in Heidegger is not, as Jean Wahl says 'the impossibility of possibility,' but 'the possibility of impossibility.' This apparently Byzantine distinction has a fundamental importance" (TA 92n5/TO 70n43). Levinas refers, in several of his works, to Heidegger's own description of death in *Being and Time* as "the possibility of impossibility" to describe his reading of death in Heidegger's *Being and Time*. For instance, in a discussion published in Wahl's book *A Short History of Existentialism* Levinas writes that authentic Being-towards-death is possibility *par excellence* because all other possibilities become acts, whereas death becomes nonbeing. "That is the sense," Levinas continues, "in which Heidegger says that death is the possibility of impossibility" (PHE 89/SHE 53). Levinas does not concede—at least in those passages where Heidegger is named explicity—the possibility that death in Heidegger's *Being and Time* is to be read as both "the possibility of impossibility" and "the impossibility of possibility." The latter phrase—"the impossibility of possibility"—articulates, according to Levinas, the fact that death is the impossibility of grasping the possible. "What is important about the approach of death is that at a certain moment we are no longer *able to be able* [*nous ne pouvons plus pouvoir*]. It is exactly thus that the subject loses its very mastery as a subject" (TA 62/TO 74). The step beyond inauthenticity into authenticity that would ensure the virility of the subject and complete fundamental ontology is interrupted. At the very moment the subject gains mastery, he or she is impotent. The production or performance of this necessary yet impossible step beyond articulates the trace of death as that which merely approaches. This approach of death indicates, according to Levinas, that one is in relation with the absolutely other (TA 63/TO 74).

Blanchot's reading of death in Heidegger's *Being and Time* is (at least up to a point) not unlike Levinas's. In a passage from *The Space of Literature* that is obviously a reading of Heidegger, Blanchot explicitly refers to Levinas's reading of Heidegger in *Time and the Other*.

> When a contemporary philosopher names death as man's extreme possibility, the possibility absolutely proper to him, he shows that the origin of possibility is linked in man to the fact that he *can* die, that for him death is yet one possibility more, that the event by which man departs from the possible and belongs to the impossible is nevertheless within his mastery, that it is the extreme moment of his possibility. (And this the philosopher expresses precisely by saying of death that it is "the possibility of impossibility.") [A footnote here reads: "Emmanuel Levinas is the first to have brought out what was at stake in this expression (*Time and the Other*)."] (EL 325–26/SL 240)

The passage continues with Blanchot establishing the proximity of this reading of death in the work of Heidegger to the work of Hegel.

> Hegel had already seen action, language, liberty, and death to be aspects of one and the same movement; he had shown that only man's constant and resolute proximity to death allows him to become active nothingness capable of negating and transforming natural reality—of combat-

ing, of laboring, of knowing, and of being historical. This is a magical force: it is the absolute power of the negative which becomes the action of truth in the world. It brings negation to reality, form to the formless, definition to the indefinite. We want to draw these limits, mark these ends, come to the finish. That is the principle behind civilization's demands, the essence of the purposeful will which seeks achievement, which demands accomplishment and attains universal mastery. Existence is authentic when it is capable of enduring possibility right up to its extreme point, able to stride toward death as toward possibility par excellence. It is to this movement that the essence of man in Western history owes its having become action, value, future, labor and truth. The affirmation that in man all is possibility requires that death itself be possible: death itself, without which man would not be able to form the notion of an "all" or to exist in view of a totality, must be what makes all—what makes totality—possible. (EL 326/SL 240)

For Hegel, death is productive. It is the effectuation of the appearance of the next shape of the dialectic. It is the possibility of each step of the dialectic that progresses ever so diligently to the notion of an "all," to absolute knowing. In another passage from *The Space of Literature*, Blanchot extends this reading of death as possibility to encompass not only Heidegger and Hegel, but also Nietzsche: "The decision to be without being is possibility itself: the possibility of death. Three systems of thought—Hegel's, Nietzsche's, Heidegger's—which attempt to account for this decision and which therefore seem, however much they may oppose each other, to shed the greatest light on the destiny of modern man, are all attempts at making death possible" (EL 115/SL 96). While it is not particularly unusual to characterize Hegel's work as a "system" of thought, the characterization seems wholly inappropriate when applied to the work of Nietzsche and Heidegger. I would suggest that Blanchot applies this characterization to one specific reading of the work of these three thinkers—a reading which reads death as *merely* possibility. Such a (limited) reading of the work of Hegel, Nietzsche, and Heidegger would, perhaps, look like this: In Hegel, death traditionally has been read as a necessary moment in the progression of Spirit through the different forms of consciousness to absolute knowing. For Hegel, death is productive. It is the effectuation of the appearance of the next shape of the dialectic. In Nietzsche, as well, death is the possibility of the step beyond. The overman, as the one free for the possibility of death, as the one who maintains the pure essence of will in willing nothingness, is the decisive step beyond the nihilism of *ressentiment*, the bad conscience, and the ascetic ideal. In Heidegger the authentic, resolute, determinate, and decided assumption of death is the step that would complete the existential analysis of Dasein.

/

Blanchot, however, like Levinas (and Derrida), thinks that such a reading of death overlooks the profoundly disturbing questionableness at the heart of this phenomenon—death as the possibility of impossibility turning into death as the impossibility of possibility, death as possibility turning into death as impossibility, that is, turning into death as the impossibility of dying. This reading of death acknowledges the power of death, while, at the same time, exposing the powerlessness of death. This reading of death (though not in every case is it a reading explicitly produced by Levinas) exposes that *moment* when death as possibility turns into the impossibility (within a Hegelian context) of producing the progressive steps of the dialectic, the impossibility (within a Nietzschean context) of effecting the decisive step of the overman, and finally, the impossibility (within a Heideggerian context) of the step that completes the existential analysis of Dasein. Here one sees a step beyond that is, *at the same time*, not beyond. Here one sees the ruination of a step *in the performance of the step itself*. Here one sees the unworking of the work.

Death possesses a genealogy and calls for being read accordingly. At a certain moment (in history) it seems as though impossibility as death is possible. But this moment is not unambiguous. A reading of death that exposes that moment when death as possibility turns into death as impossibility calls the initial reading of death (as possibility) into question, thereby calling for a reading that necessarily, yet impossibly, thinks together death as possibility and death as impossibility.

This genealogy of death will be explored throughout this chapter with respect to the work of Levinas. The genealogy of death not only opens up new and provocative readings of the work of Levinas, but it also raises the question of the proximity of his work to the work of Hegel, Nietzsche, and Heidegger (as well as Blanchot and Derrida), oftentimes despite Levinas's expressed intentions.

A few prefatory remarks are in order. The question of the proximity of the work of Levinas and other thinkers is raised with respect to the moment when death as possibility turns into death as impossibility. At this moment, if only for a moment, one can think together the work Levinas and other thinkers of death as (im)possibility. This is not done out of ignorance of the essential differences between the thinkers. It is not done out of ignorance of the different horizons of thought from which their works emerge. It is done with an attentiveness to those decisive moments in their work when work is discovered to be at a certain distance from that work.

One of the most predominant readings of Heidegger's *Being and Time* has come to be known as the "existential" reading. The existential analysis of

Dasein, undertaken in the name of fundamental ontology, is rigorously delimited by the crucial distinction between inauthenticity and authenticity. The existential reading of *Being and Time* reads this distinction, I would suggest, *as* a distinction, that is, *as* two separate, distinguishable ways of being. This reading reads the task of the existential analysis and, therefore, fundamental ontology, as merely a step beyond inauthenticity into authenticity. The analysis of death that opens the second division of *Being and Time* affirms, according to the existential reading, the possibility of the existential analysis by affirming the possibility of completing this step, that is, by bringing to light Dasein's authentic potentiality-for-Being-a-whole. "By pointing out that Dasein has an *authentic potentiality-for-Being-a-whole*, the existential analytic acquires assurance as to the constitution of Dasein's *primordial* Being" (SZ 234/BT 277). Death is the possibility that completes the step, it is the possibility that discloses Dasein's authentic potentiality-for-Being-a-whole. But this reading—a reading that reads death *merely* as possibility—repeats the most familiar and traditional of steps.

The analysis of death in *Being and Time* arises in response to the question of whether or not the existential analysis of Dasein undertaken in division 1 is complete, whether or not it has grasped Dasein as a whole. But this demand for the completion of the existential analysis seems "manifestly inconsistent" (SZ 236/BT 279) with the analysis of care which forms the structural whole of Dasein. The "primary item" in the structure of care is the "ahead-of-itself" (*Sichvorweg*), which harkens back to the potentiality-for-Being (*Seinkönnen*) central to the analysis of understanding (*Verstehen*) (SZ 236/BT 279). The ahead-of-itself indicates that in Dasein there is always something still outstanding that, as a potentiality-for-Being for Dasein, has not yet become "actual" (SZ 236/BT 279). The inconsistency, therefore, is this: as soon as Dasein is wholly itself, Dasein is not. As soon as there is no longer anything still outstanding, then Dasein is "no-longer-Being-there" (*Nicht-mehr-da-sein*), that is, Dasein is no longer (SZ 236/BT 280). But rather than simply preclude the analysis of death, this inconsistency—the necessary yet impossible coincidence of being and nonbeing—forms, as will become apparent throughout the course of the analysis, the element of the death analysis that calls for thinking.

Heidegger then establishes, within the context of an analysis of the possibility of experiencing the death of others, that death is not merely an event (*Begebenheit*). In the wake of the seeming inconsistency of Dasein itself getting access to the phenomenon of death, this analysis arises as an alternative means of getting access to the phenomenon. But Heidegger concludes that despite the fact that Dasein can be represented by another (SZ 239/BT 283), the possibility of representing breaks down completely in the phenomenon of death. "*No one can take the Other's dying away from him*" (SZ 240/BT 284).

I am, with respect to the phenomenon of death, unrepresentable. This impossibility of substitution is due to the mineness (*Jemeinigkeit*) of death. Heidegger than writes that death is not an event, but rather a phenomenon that is to be understood existentially (SZ 240/BT 284).

In order to get a genuinely existential conception of the phenomenon of death, it is necessary, therefore, to determine the way that death belongs to existence. According to the analysis of the structure of care, Dasein's existence consists in its being always already "ahead of itself." Dasein always already projects ahead to what it *not yet* is. It always already is its not yet. And just as it always already is its not yet, it always already is its end also. Yet the ending that Heidegger has in view in his analysis of death does not indicate Dasein's Being-at-an-end (*Zu-Ende-sein*), but rather Dasein's Being-towards-the-end (*Sein zum Ende*) (SZ 245/BT 289). Therefore, the not-yet of death, considered existentially, has the character of something toward which Dasein comports itself. Death, Heidegger writes, is something impending (*Bevorstand*) (SZ 250/BT 293–94). In fact, it is a possibility that is distinctively impending in that it is not simply a being but also, and at the same time, non-being.

At this point in the work, the careful and rigorous analysis has dramatically arrived at the moment of what seems to be its fulfillment. The essence of Dasein, the being proper to Dasein, is the being-possible (*das Möglichsein*). A thinking of the possible guides the existential analysis of death. In fact, a certain thinking of the possible is the hinge upon which not only the existential analysis of death turns, but also (by implication) the hinge upon which the task of the existential analysis of Dasein and, therefore, fundamental ontology, turns. A certain thinking of the possible is the hinge that both opens and closes this "work." "This possibility of the possible," as Derrida notes in *Aporias*, "brings together *on the one hand* the sense of the virtuality or of the imminence of the future, of the 'that can always happen at any instant,' one *must expect it, I am expecting it, we are expecting it,* and *on the other hand*, the sense of ability, of the possible as that of which I am capable, that for which I have the power, the ability, or the potentiality" (AM 332/AD 62). Possibility (*die Möglichkeit*) encompasses both of these meanings.

Certain statements in Heidegger's existential analysis characterize death as Dasein's most proper possibility. The being proper to Dasein is being-possible, and the most proper possibility of this possibility is death. But this most proper possibility of Dasein is not a characteristic to be registered. It must be assumed; these statements of the existential analysis are prescriptive. These statements give rise to the existential reading of the analysis of death offered (in certain passages and certain texts) by Levinas and Blanchot. These statements give rise to a reading of death as possibility. For example, Levinas (in a passage quoted earlier) writes that being toward death "is *Dasein's* assumption

of the uttermost possibility of existence, which precisely makes possible all
other possibilities, and consequently makes possible the very feat of grasping
a possibility—that is, it makes possible activity and freedom" (TA 57/TO 70).
Blanchot writes (again in a passage quoted earlier): "When a contemporary
philosopher names death as man's extreme possibility, the possibility
absolutely proper to him, he shows that the origin of possibility is linked in
man to the fact that he *can* die, that for him death is yet one possibility more,
that the event by which man departs from the possible and belongs to the
impossible is nevertheless within his mastery, that it is the extreme moment of
his possibility" (EL 325–26/SL 240). One such prescriptive statement is situated in the heart of the existential analysis of death in *Being and Time*: "Death
is a possibility-of-Being [*Seinsmöglichkeit*] which Dasein itself has to take
over [*zu übernehmen*] in every case. With death, Dasein stands before itself
[*steht sich . . . bevor*] in its ownmost potentiality-for-Being [*in seinem eigen-
sten Seinkönnen*]" (SZ 250/BT 294). Death is a possibility that can and must
be *assumed*. Death is a possibility that Dasein has always to take over—that is,
a possibility upon which, using terminology introduced in the analysis of
understanding, Dasein must project itself (see especially SZ 142–48/BT
182–88). In fact, it is the only possibility upon which Dasein has no choice but
to project itself. Projecting itself upon this possibility Dasein stands before
itself in its potentiality-for-Being—that is, it is given back to itself, disclosed
to itself, from that possibility. This possibility is Dasein's *ownmost* possibility
(Heidegger's analysis will demonstrate that this is Dasein's ownmost possibility in that projection upon this possibility opens up the space of ownness).

This first series of statements—which give rise to a reading of death as
possibility—is, however, supplemented by another series of statements.
"This second series," Derrida writes in *Aporias*, "is an aporetic supplement
because it is in the same sentence, in the interrupted unity of the same propo-
sitional syntax in a way, that the impossibility adds an impossible complement, a complement of impossibility to possibility" (AM 333/AD 67–68).
Possibility and impossibility are, like the two moments of an irreducibly
ambiguous double reading, the "two moments of a single aporetic sentence"
(AM 332/AD 64). Precisely insofar as death is Dasein's most proper being-
possible (in both senses of the word), it is at the same time the possibility of
an impossibility. How does this "aporetic supplement" affect the existential
analytic? How, if at all, is one to assume this aporetically supplemented possibility? There are several examples of this supplementation. One occurs
immediately after the example of death as Dasein's most proper possibility
quoted above. This aporetic supplement dogs this first statement's step.

This is a possibility in which the issue is nothing less than Dasein's
Being-in-the-world [*In-der-Welt-sein*]. Its death is the possibility of no-

longer-being-able-to-be-there [*die Möglichkeit des Nicht-mehr-dasein-könnens*]. If Dasein stands before itself [*seiner selbst sich bevorsteht*] as this possibility, it has been *fully* assigned [*verwiesen*] to its ownmost potentiality-for-Being [*eigenstes Seinkönnen*]. When it stands before itself in this way, all its relations to any other Dasein have been undone. (SZ 250/BT 294)

What is at issue for Dasein in its projection upon this possibility, and its being disclosed to itself from this possibility, is, as the analysis of anxiety shows, nothing within-the-world but rather being-in-the-world as such. What is at issue is Dasein's no-longer-being-able-to-be-there. What is more, not only does this projection and self-disclosure banish Dasein from present-at-hand and ready-to-hand entities within-the-world, it exiles Dasein *fully*, that is, it undoes the Dasein-with of others. To project upon this possibility and to be disclosed from it—that is, to stand before itself—is to be in utter exile. This possibility is *non-relational*. Derrida notes a nuance in the statement that death is "the possibility of no-longer-being-able-to-be-there." The possibility of no-longer-being-able-to-be-there is the *possibility* of a being-able-not-to or the *possibility* of a no-longer-being-able-to, but it is not the *impossibility* of a being-able-to. The very fragility of this nuance not only is both "decisive and significant," but also, probably is "most essential" in Heidegger's view (AM 334/AD 68). This nuance speaks (if one is permitted to assume that "no-longer-being-able-to" can be read as "impossibility") of the possibility of impossibility, not the impossibility of possibility. Hence Heidegger adds a few sentences later: "This ownmost non-relational [*unbezügliche*] possibility is at the same time the uttermost one [*die äußerste*]. As potentiality-for-Being, Dasein cannot outstrip [*überholen*] the possibility of death. Death is the possibility of the absolute impossibility of Dasein" (SZ 250/BT 294). This part of the passage follows almost directly from the previous parts—since death is Dasein's ownmost, non-relational possibility, it is the extreme possibility. Death is that possibility that circumscribes all possibilities. This possibility is *unsurpassable, not to be outstripped*. The nuance noted by Derrida raises certain questions about Levinas's reading of the existential analysis of death. Recall that Levinas draws the following "apparently Byzantine distinction" (though one of "fundamental importance"): death in Heidegger is not the impossibility of possibility, but the possibility of impossibility. The phrase *the impossibility of possibility* articulates, for Levinas (and Blanchot), the fact that death is the limit of the subject's activity and mastery. Is death in the work of Levinas—written as the impossibility of possibility—merely opposed to death in the work of Heidegger? The response to these questions is better left deferred until after the truly aporetic character of Heidegger's analysis is brought to the fore. (It should be noted, before moving on, that Heidegger himself reverses the order of presentation; see SZ 265/BT 310.) Heidegger repeats this aporetic supplement to the first statement several times later in the analysis. However, it is necessary to set the stage for these statements.

The three determinations of death that have emerged so far from the analysis are gathered together: "Thus *death* reveals itself as that *possibility which is one's ownmost, which is non-relational, and which is not to be out-stripped*. As such, death is something *distinctively* impending" (SZ 250–51/BT 294). The possibility of death is distinctive in that it is otherwise than any impending possibility *within*-the-world. The passage continues by emphasizing that the possibility of death is not only a mode of disclosedness, but, in a certain sense, a privileged mode. "Its existential possibility is based on the fact that Dasein is essentially disclosed [*erschlossen*] to itself, and dis-closed, indeed, as ahead-of-itself [*Sich-vorweg*]. This item in the structure of care has its most primordial concretion in Being-towards-death" (SZ 251/BT 294). According to the analysis of the structure of care, Dasein's existence consists in its being always already "ahead of itself." Being-towards-death is the most originary concretion of this moment in the structure of care.

Having determined the way that death belongs to existence, the analy-sis is extended to include the other two moments in the structure of care: thrownness (*Geworfenheit*) and falling (*Verfallen*). Dasein always already finds itself in relation to that possibility upon which it projects in Being-towards-death. "This ownmost possibility, however, non-relational and not to be outstripped, is not one which Dasein procures for itself subsequently and occasionally [*nachträglich und gelegentlich*] in the course of its Being. On the contrary, if Dasein exists, it has already been *thrown* into this possibility" (SZ 251/BT 295). But despite the fact that Dasein is thrown into this possibility, it can and for the most part does cover up or evade what gets disclosed from projection upon this possibility. It falls away from such disclosure: "[P]roxi-mally and for the most part Dasein covers up its ownmost Being-towards-death, fleeing *in the face* of it" (SZ 251/BT 295).

The analysis of falling sets the stage for an extended analysis of every-day Being-towards-death that in turn sets the stage for the analysis of the final trait(s) of the full existential conception of death. The other trait(s) address(es) the certitude of death. Death is certain, but there is something peculiar (*eigen-tümlich*) in its certainty. For the certainty of death is always already accom-panied by an "indefiniteness" with respect to its "when" (SZ 258/BT 302). Death is an indefinite certainty. "Nowhere does Heidegger's project veer so close to its Cartesian legacy; nowhere does it repudiate that legacy so deci-sively."[1] This is echoed in the work of Levinas on death, which, I have sug-gested, is to be read alongside his reading of Descartes' *Meditations*.

The analysis also is extended to a consideration of authentic Being-towards-death. "*Authentic* Being-towards-death can *not evade* its ownmost non-relational possibility, or *cover up* this possibility by thus fleeing from it, or *give a new explanation* for it to accord with the common sense of the 'they'" (SZ 260/BT 304–5). Authentic Being-towards-death is a comportment to death as possibility; it lets death be as possibility: "[I]t must be understood *as a possibility*, it must be cultivated *as a possibility*, and we must *put up with* it *as a possibility*, in the way we comport ourselves towards it" (SZ 261/BT 306). Being out for something concernfully, brooding, and expecting are all ways of being toward a possibility that flee in the face of possibility as possibility. Heidegger writes that being out for something concernfully and expecting look away from the possible to its possible actualization, while brooding weakens possibility by calculating how one can have it at one's disposal. Being toward the possibility of death *as a possibility* is anticipation (*Vorlaufen*) of this possibility.

Recall that certain statements in Heidegger's existential analysis supplement the characterization of death as Dasein's most proper possibility with impossibility: "Death is the possibility of the absolute impossibility of Dasein" (SZ 250/BT 294). Heidegger repeats this aporetic statement several times. "The more unveiledly this possibility gets understood [*Je unverhüllter diese Möglichkeit verstanden wird*], the more purely [*um so reiner*] does the understanding penetrate into it [*dringt . . . vor*] as the possibility of the impossibility of any existence at all [*als die der Unmöglichkeit der Existenz überhaupt*]" (SZ 262/BT 307). What is both unveiled and unveiled by, for, and during a penetrating advance, is this possibility *as possibility of* the impossibility, this possibility *as* impossibility, this *most proper* possibility of Dasein *as* its proper impossibility (hence, the *least proper*, says Derrida, not Heidegger). The text then, Derrida notes, "imperceptibly moves" from the "possibility *as possibility of* the impossibility" to the "possibility *of* impossibility" (AM 335/AD 71). There are at least two examples of this move in the following passage:

> Death, as possibility, gives Dasein nothing to be 'actualized' [*nichts zu »Verwirklichendes«*], nothing which Dasein, as actual, could itself *be*. It [i.e., death] is the possibility of the impossibility [*die Möglichkeit der Unmöglichkeit*] of every way of comporting oneself towards anything, of every way of existing. In the anticipation of this possibility it becomes 'greater and greater' [*»immer größer«*]; that is to say, the possibility reveals itself [*enthüllt sich*] to be such that it knows no measure at all, no more or less, but signifies the possibility of the measureless impossibility of existence [*die Möglichkeit der maßlosen Unmöglichkeit der Existenz*]. (SZ 262/BT 307)

Death is not one example among many of the aporetic supplement of impossibility by impossibility. It is the unique occurrence, the unique production, of this aporia: the possibility of impossibility. It is unique because what is at issue is not a particular possibility or impossibility within the world, but *being-in-the-world* as such, existence as such. "Any other determined possibility or impossibility would take on meaning and would be defined within its limits in terms of this particular possibility of impossibility, *this* particular impossibility" (AM 335/AD 72). The preceding passage from *Being and Time* announces the "as such" (*als solche*) central to Derrida's reading. Derrida's translation (or more precisely, the English translation of Derrida's translation) is slightly different than the Macquarrie and Robinson translation. Derrida's translation brings out the "as such" as such. "In the anticipation of this possibility, it becomes 'greater and greater,' that is to say, the possibility reveals itself *as such* [*als solche*], it reveals itself to be such that it knows no measure at all, no more or less, but signifies the possibility of the measureless impossibility of existence (SZ 262/BT 307, emphasis added; see AM 335/AD 71–72)."[2] Everything turns on the enigma of the as such. This is apparent at what I would suggest is the heart of Derrida's reading of Heidegger's existential analysis of death, which calls for a close, careful, and detailed reading. It is a matter of nuance.

Heidegger says that for Dasein (and for Dasein alone) impossibility as death is possible, that is, can appear as such and announce itself. Dasein alone is capable of this aporia. "And," Derrida adds in *Aporias*, "it is only in the act of authentic (*eigentlich*), resolute, determinate, and decided assumption by which *Dasein* would take upon itself the possibility of this impossibility that the aporia *as such* would announce itself *as such* and purely to *Dasein* as its most proper possibility, hence as the most proper essence of *Dasein*, its freedom, its ability to question, and its opening to the meaning of being" (AM 336/AD 74–75). Here Derrida asks the possible/impossible question that sets the stage for the ruinous performance of the necessary yet impossible step beyond into authenticity that is at the heart of the possibility of the existential analysis: what difference is there between the possibility of appearing as such of the possibility of an impossibility and the *im*possibility of appearing as such of the possibility of an impossibility (AM 336/AD 75)? Paralleling the first part of this possible/impossible question, Derrida writes: "According to Heidegger, it is therefore the impossibility of the 'as such' that, *as such, would be possible* to Dasein" (AM 336/AD 75, emphasis added to "would be possible"), would appear as such to Dasein. It is important to note that this step remains this side of ruination. It remains, as Derrida noted earlier, the act of authentic, resolute, determinate, and decided assumption by which Dasein would take upon itself the possibility of this impossibility. But then a "but" announces a change in nuance. Paralleling the second part of the possible/impossible question, Derrida writes: "But if the impossibility of the as such is indeed the impossibility of the 'as such' [i.e., if the impossibility of the as such is *indeed impossible*], it [i.e., the impossibility of the as such] is *also* what cannot appear as such" (AM 336/AD 75, emphasis added), is *also* what *would not be possible* to Dasein, contrary—and is it contrary?—to what is said in the step performed just prior to the "but." "Indeed," Derrida adds, "this relation to the disappearing as such of the 'as such'—the 'as such' that Heidegger makes the distinctive mark and the specific ability of *Dasein* [i.e., the authentic, resolute, determinate, and decided assumption of the possibility of the impossibility of death]—is also the characteristic common *both* to the inauthentic *and* to the authentic forms of the existence of *Dasein*" (AM 336/AD 75). The fact that the impossibility that *would be possible* to Dasein (in authentic existence) cannot appear as such, that is, *would not be possible* to Dasein (even in authentic existence) erases the distinction between the inauthentic (in which impossibility as death does *not* appear as such, is evaded) and the authentic (in which impossibility as death *supposedly* can appear). Here one sees the ruination of the step that would complete the existential analysis *in the performance of the step itself.* Here one sees the unworking of the work.

With this reading in *Aporias*, Derrida shows how what is at the very heart of the possibility of the existential analysis of death as possibility of the impossibility of the Dasein can be turned against the very possibility of the existential analysis, depending on the way one reads the expression "the possibility of impossibility" (AM 336–37/AD 76–77). This is the context of Derrida's remark that "[w]hen Blanchot constantly repeats—and it is a long complaint and not a triumph of life—the impossible dying, the impossibility, alas, of dying, he says at once the same thing and something completely different from Heidegger" (AM 337/AD 77). Turning what is at the very heart of the possibility of the existential analysis of death, that is, the appropriation of death, against the very possibility of the existential analysis, Derrida writes: "If death, the most proper possibility of *Dasein*, is the possibility of its impossibility, death becomes the most improper possibility and the most ex-propriating, the most inauthenticating one" (AM 337/AD 77). That certain statements in Heidegger's existential analysis supplement the characterization of death as Dasein's most proper possibility with impossibility ("Death is the possibility of the absolute impossibility of Dasein") is (depending on how one reads the expression "the possibility of impossibility") what Blanchot, in *The Space of Literature*, calls "double death" (*la double mort*).

The first movement of this doubling is marked by Dasein's return to itself. Projection upon and disclosure from this possibility serve to draw Dasein back from dispersion to a certain unity with itself, to a certain wholeness. This possibility—which marks the condition of the possibility of possibility—discloses Dasein in its ownmost.

The second movement of this doubling effects an interruption of the first movement. For that possibility which discloses Dasein in its ownmost is, at the same time, the possibility that banishes Dasein to utter exile, that separates it not only from others and the world, but also from itself, from all that it could be, since it cannot simply be dead. "One sees, then, that the coincidence of being and nonbeing, inscribed in the analysis of death from the outset, even, in a sense, *producing* that analysis, comes to be reinscribed at the end of the analysis as the coincidence of ownmost and othermost."[3] This possibility marks not only the condition of the possibility of possibility, but at the same time, the condition of the impossibility of possibility. On the one hand, death (as possibility) effects the possibility of completing the existential analysis, insofar as the task of the existential analysis is understood as a step beyond inauthenticity into authenticity (a step that is the most familiar and traditional of steps). But, on the other hand, death (as impossibility) is ruinous of not only the possibility of the existential analysis (insofar as it is understood as merely a step from the inauthentic to the authentic), but also, of the very language of possibility itself—death as possibility turning into death as impossibility. One is here called to think together that which is impossible to think together—Dasein *is* (being) and *is not* (nonbeing), it is itself in being other, it is ownmost and othermost, it is homecoming in exile.[4]

In both "The Trace of the Other" and "Meaning and Sense" Levinas implicitly casts Heidegger's philosophy as one ultimately characterized by homecoming. For example, in a passage from "Meaning and Sense"—a passage whose context obviously indicates that he is referring, among other philosophers, to Heidegger—Levinas writes: "Philosophy's itinerary remains that of Ulysses, whose adventure in the world was only a return to his native island—a complacency in the Same, an unrecognition of the other" (SS 43/MS 91). However, Levinas wishes to oppose the story of Abraham to the myth of Ulysses. In "The Trace of the Other" he writes: "To the myth of Ulysses returning to Ithaca, we wish to oppose the story of Abraham who leaves his fatherland forever for a yet unknown land, and forbids his servant to even bring back his son to the point of departure" (TdA 191/ToO 348). Levinas's choice of the word *oppose* is perhaps a bit too polemical since the relation of homecoming to exile can never be one merely of opposition.

As mentioned earlier, there are moments in the work of Blanchot that attend to the moment when death as possibility turns into death as impossibility. What follows are instances of this moment in Blanchot's reading of Hegel and Nietzsche. Again, this reading is not produced with an eye to minimizing the differences between the work of Hegel and that of Nietzsche (or between any of the thinkers of death as (im)possibility, or even between the various works of

Blanchot himself).[5] The question of the proximity of the work of these thinkers is raised, despite their differences, with respect to the moment when death as possibility turns into death as impossibility. At this moment, if only for a moment, one can think together these thinkers of death as (im)possibility.

The doubling of death considered earlier first appears in Blanchot's work in a reading of Hegel in "Literature and the Right to Death." "[L]itera-ture begins at the moment when literature becomes a question" (LDM 293/LRD 21). This question—"the 'question' that seeks to pose itself in liter-ature, the 'question' that is its essence" (LDM 311/LRD 41)—is posed *to* lan-guage *by* language that has become literature. This question is "an irreducible *double meaning* [*un double sens irréductible*]" (LDM 330/LRD 61): death as possibility and as impossibility. "Literature," Blanchot writes in the conclud-ing sentence of the essay, "is the form this double meaning has chosen in which to show itself behind the meaning and value of words, and the question it asks is the question asked by literature" (LDM 331/LRD 62). This question is what Blanchot, in *The Space of Literature*, calls "double death."

The following remarks on "Literature and the Right to Death" are lim-ited to a reading of two of what Blanchot calls a "writer's temptations." A writer's temptations are those decisive moments in the *Phenomenology of Spirit*, those "decisive moments in history" (LDM 309/LRD 38), which *seem* (at least on a first reading) to describe the very process of literary creation, the destructive act of transformation. But these decisive moments are fraught with ambiguity. One temptation—"revolution" or "revolutionary action"—marks the first instance of Blanchot's irreducibly ambiguous reading of the follow-ing passage from the preface to Hegel's *Phenomenology of Spirit*: "[T]he life of Spirit is [. . .] the life that endures it [i.e., death] and maintains itself in it" (PG 27/PS 19). Literature begins at the moment when it becomes a question, that is, at the moment when an initial reading of this passage, which reads death as possibility, turns into a reading of this passage that reads death as impossibility. Death, as this turning *itself*, leaves a trace of itself, I would sug-gest, in the production or performance of an interminable step/not beyond (*le pas au-delà*). This reading of "revolution" or "revolutionary action" will raise the question of the proximity of this temptation and Blanchot's reading in *The Infinite Conversation* of nihilism in the work of Nietzsche. Nihilism is another temptation of a writer named by Blanchot in "Literature and the Right to Death."

In the first part of "Literature and the Right to Death"—the part that cul-minates in a reading of revolution or revolutionary action as one of a writer's temptations—Blanchot reads the experience of the writer alongside the expe-rience of natural consciousness in Hegel's *Phenomenology of Spirit*. Or more precisely, he rewrites the experience of natural consciousness as an experience of a writer. For example, Blanchot describes work—citing an interpretation offered by Kojève in his *Introduction to the Reading of Hegel: Lectures on the Phenomenology of Spirit*—as the realization of a plan through a process of transformation. It is a production that effectuates the appearance of something (recall the role of production in the work of Levinas). Blanchot uses the example of making a stove in order to get warm. The production of an actual stove both *affirms* the presence of something that was not there before and *denies* the presence of something that was there before. The stones and cast iron are transformed—that is, denied or negated—in the work of transforming an empty ideal into something real. This new object that changes the world in turn will change the producer. This transformative act of production that is the negation of the former condition of the world and the preparation of its future is, according to Hegel and Marx, the formation of history. Reading this interpretation of Hegel alongside the experience of a writer, Blanchot writes: "If we see work as the force of history, the force that transforms man while it transforms the world, then a writer's activity must be recognized as the highest form of work" (LDM 304/LRD 33). The writer's transformative act of production is limitless. The writer can write anything. Everything is instantly accessible to the writer. Even an enslaved writer, given only a few moments of freedom in which to write, can *immediately* give himself or herself a world of freedom. But there is a ruination of action in this action. At decisive moments in the activity of literature, literature confronts the impossibility of work. The writer ruins action not because he or she deals with what is unreal, but because he or she makes *all* of reality available. The unreal realm of the imaginary is not situated beyond the world, but is the world itself as a whole. This realm is not in the world because it is the world realized in its entirety by the "global negation" of all the individual realities contained in the world. This global negation of all the individual realities is the realization of that absence itself (LDM 307/LRD 36). Here the movement of negation characteristic of the transformative act of production is the endeavor to realize that "movement of negation" itself. Literature, like every other activity in the world, presupposes the "movement of comprehension," the movement of negation. But literature endeavors to realize or produce (that is, effectuate the appearance of) this very movement itself. Blanchot articulates this endeavor in various ways and in various locations throughout "Literature and the Right to Death." For example: "Literature is not content to accept only the fragmentary, successive results of this movement of negation: it wants to grasp the movement itself and it wants to comprehend the results in their totality" (LDM 319/LRD 48–49). Literature endeavors to step into that which is the very condition of any step of literature. Blanchot attends to the moment when literature, understood as a particular activity in the world, endeavors to disclose to itself the condition of literature. However, this endeavor is tragic because the power of negation, death, is the blind spot of language.

Whoever sees God dies.[6] In speech what dies is what gives life to speech; speech is the life of that death, it is "the life that endures death and maintains itself in it." What wonderful power. But something was there and is no longer there. Something has disappeared. How can I recover it, how can I turn around and look at what exists *before*, if all my power consists of making it into what exists *after*? The language of literature is a search for this moment which precedes literature. (LDM 316/LRD 46)

Literature realizes, in its tragic endeavor "to become the revelation of what revelation destroys" (LDM 317/LRD 47), that its "step beyond" is inevitably "not beyond." In a passage that perhaps recalls Heidegger's remarks on the term *own* (*eigen*), Blanchot writes that literature "learns that it cannot go beyond itself toward its *own* end" (LDM 318/LRD 47, emphasis added), toward its ownmost possibility—the movement of negation *itself*. One can step beyond stepping into the very possibility of stepping itself only by stepping; that is, the step beyond inevitably reinscribes one in stepping. This tragic step, this step/not beyond (*le pas au-delà*), is the articulation, according to Blanchot, of those decisive moments in the work or production of the *Phenomenology of Spirit* when work or production is discovered to be at a certain distance from that work.

One of those decisive moments in the *Phenomenology of Spirit* is, according to Blanchot, "revolution." "Revolution" or "revolutionary action" is what Blanchot calls one of a writer's temptations. A writer's temptations are those decisive moments in the *Phenomenology of Spirit*, those "decisive moments in history" (LDM 309/LRD 38), which *seem* (at least on a first reading) to describe the very process of literary creation, the destructive act of transformation that is a step into the next stage of the dialectical progression. But these decisive moments are ambiguous. Blanchot reads the experience of the writer alongside that moment of the *Phenomenology of Spirit* titled "Absolute Freedom and Terror." In the writer, Blanchot writes, "negation [. . .] wishes to realize itself" (LDM 308/LRD 38). Blanchot continues:

It is at this point that he encounters those decisive moments in history when everything seems put in question, when law, faith, the State, the world above, the world of the past—everything sinks effortlessly, without work, into nothingness. The man knows he has not stepped out of history, but history is now the void, the void in the process of realization; it is *absolute* freedom which has become an event. Such periods are given the name Revolution. At this moment, freedom aspires to be realized in the *immediate* form of *everything* is possible, everything can be done. (LDM 309/LRD 38)

The fabulous moment in history when one experiences his or her "*own* free-dom as *universal* freedom" (LDM 309/LRD 38, emphasis added) ushers in the Reign of Terror, for the decision to allow the universality of freedom to assert itself completely in him or her negates the particular reality of his or her life (LDM 310/LRD 39). The meaning of the Reign of Terror is this: every cit-izen has a "right to death." Every citizen has a right to death because it is with death that absolute freedom is realized (recall that Dasein's assumption of its *own*most possibility is a "*freedom towards death*"; SZ 266/BT 311). But it is precisely at this decisive moment in history that death as possibility turns into death as impossibility. At this decisive moment Blanchot introduces, for the first time in his work, the distinction between death as possibility and death as impossibility.

> Death as an event no longer has any importance. During the Reign of Terror individuals die and it means nothing. In the famous words of Hegel, "It is thus the coldest and meanest of all deaths, with no more sig-nificance than cutting off a head of cabbage or swallowing a mouthful of water." Why? Isn't death the achievement of freedom—that is, the rich-est moment of meaning? But it is also only the empty point in that free-dom, a manifestation of the fact that such a freedom is still abstract, ideal (literary), that it is only poverty and platitude. (LDM 310/LRD 39–40)

At this decisive moment in the *Phenomenology of Spirit*, in history, death as possibility, as the "richest moment of meaning," is discovered to be at a cer-tain distance from the *Phenomenology of Spirit*, from history. It is discovered to be interrupted, or said otherwise, to be weakened—death as impossibility. It is at this decisive moment in history that a reading of the following passage from the preface to the *Phenomenology of Spirit* becomes irreducibly ambigu-ous: "[T]he life of Spirit is [. . .] the life that endures it [i.e., death] and main-tains itself in it." Blanchot writes: "Literature contemplates itself in revolu-tion, it finds its justification in revolution, and if it has been called the Reign of Terror, this is because its ideal is indeed that moment in history, that moment when 'life endures death and maintains itself in it' in order to gain from death the possibility of speaking and the truth of speech. This is the 'question' that seeks to pose itself in literature, the 'question' that is its essence" (LDM 311/LRD 41). Literature begins at the moment when it becomes a question, that is, at the moment when an initial reading of the pas-sage "life endures death and maintains itself in it" that reads death as possi-bility, turns into a reading of this passage that reads death as impossibility. Death, as this turning *itself*, leaves a trace of itself, I would suggest, in the pro-duction or performance of an interminable step/not beyond (*le pas au-delà*).

Literature is the very production or performance of the ambiguous step/not beyond. What appears in this production or performance of a step/not beyond is an irreducible ambiguity of being and nothingness (LDM 327/LRD 58). Literature is the very production or performance of a trace of that which withdraws from (or, said otherwise, which infinity approaches) revelation.

This reading of revolution or revolutionary action raises the question of the proximity of this temptation and Blanchot's reading in *The Infinite Conversation* of nihilism in the work of Nietzsche. It is important to note that nihilism is another temptation of a writer named by Blanchot in "Literature and the Right to Death." Writing nihilism alongside skepticism in Hegel's *Phenomenology of Spirit*, Blanchot writes that the writer is a nihilist "because he does not simply negate this and that by methodical work which slowly transforms each thing: he negates everything at once, and he is obliged to negate everything, since he only deals with everything" (LDM 308/LRD 37). Recall that revolution is a decisive moment in history when everything is called into question. "At this moment," Blanchot writes, "freedom aspires to be realized in the *immediate* form of *everything* is possible, everything can be done" (LDM 309/LRD 38). Nihilism is likewise a decisive event in history.

> [N]ihilism is an event accomplished in history that is like a shedding of history—the moment when history turns and that is indicated by a negative trait: that values no longer have value in themselves. There is also a positive trait: for the first time the horizon is infinitely open to knowledge, "Everything is permitted." This new authorization given to man when the authority of values has collapsed means first of all: knowing everything is permitted, there is no longer a limit to man's activity. "*We have a still undiscovered country before us, the boundaries of which no one has seen, a beyond to all countries and corners of the ideal known hitherto, a world so over-rich in the beautiful, the strange, the questionable, the frightful.*" (EI 218–19/IC 145)

Blanchot's description of the achieving of this achievement, the realization of this extreme point or extreme form of nihilism, which corresponds to the movement of science (and, in turn, to the domination of the earth, EI 220/IC 146), is not unlike his description in "Literature and the Right to Death" of the destructive act of transformation, of the power of work that "realizes being in denying it, and reveals it at the end of the negation" (LDM 305/LRD 33). In *The Infinite Conversation*, Blanchot writes: "[A]ll modern humanism, the work of science, and planetary development have as their object a dissatisfaction with what is, and thus the desire to transform being—to negate it in

order to derive power from it and to make of this power to negate the infinite
movement of human mastery" (EI 225/IC 149). But this passage, which
describes the realization of the extreme point or extreme form of nihilism,
only tells half of the story. It will be necessary to return to this passage and
situate it within its proper context.

At a certain moment in history, Nietzsche writes in *On the Genealogy
of Morals*, the will to truth is revealed in its truth. When Christian truthfulness
asks itself "What is the meaning of all will to truth?" it will bring about its
own destruction through an act of self-overcoming. "All great things," Nietzsche writes, "bring about their own destruction through an act of self-overcoming [*Selbstaufhebung*]: thus the law of life will have it, the law of the
necessity of 'self-overcoming' [„*Selbstüberwindung*"] in the nature of life—
the lawgiver himself eventually receives the call: '*patere legem, quam ipse
tulisti*' ['submit to the law you yourself proposed']" (GdM 428/GoM 161).
This necessary act of self-overcoming, this *Aufhebung* that is at the threshold
of a step beyond nihilism is "weakened" by the very work of *On the Genealogy of Morals*. In response to the question "What is the meaning of all will to
truth?" the final dramatically climactic lines of the work answer: "*[W]hat* is
expressed by all that willing which has taken its direction from the ascetic
ideal" is "*a will to nothingness*, an aversion to life, a rebellion against the most
fundamental presuppositions of life; but it is and remains a *will!* . . . And, to
repeat in conclusion what I said at the beginning: man would rather will *nothingness* than *not* will" (GdM 430/GoM 162–63). The will to truth is revealed
as a will to nothingness. Here is a moment in history when history is revealed
in its truth. Here is also the prophesying of the extreme form of nihilism: the
overman as the one who maintains this pure essence of will in willing nothingness. But this *Aufhebung* that is a step beyond nihilism insofar as it reveals
a concealed evaluation as the truth of history, *repeats* the evaluative move
characteristic of nihilism thereby reinscribing the step beyond nihilism into
the not beyond. The genealogist becomes inextricably implicated in the move
of the ascetic priest. The genealogist, therefore, produces or performs a
step/not beyond (*le pas au-delà*), a step beyond that returns.

Although the eternal return remains merely implicit in the structure of
On the Genealogy of Morals, Nietzsche explicitly draws a connection
between the eternal return and nihilism in one of the notes of what was to be
The Will to Power: Attempt at a Revaluation of All Values—a text that Nietzsche refers to as a "work in progress" (GdM 427/GoM 160) in the final pages
of *On the Genealogy of Morals*.

> Let us think this thought in its most terrible form: existence as it
> is, without meaning or aim, yet recurring inevitably without any finale
> of nothingness: "*the eternal recurrence*."

> This is the most extreme form of nihilism: the nothing (the "meaningless"), eternally! (NF 217/WP 35–36)

This passage tells one that the extreme form of nihilism is precisely where the possibility of coming to an end—that is, the possibility of maintaining the pure essence of will in willing nothingness—turns into the impossibility of coming to an end.

> Until now we thought nihilism was tied to nothingness. How ill-considered this was: nihilism is tied to being. Nihilism is the impossibility of being done with it and of finding a way out even in that end that is nothingness. It says the impotence of nothingness, the false brilliance of its victories; it tells us that when we think nothingness we are still thinking being. Nothing ends, everything begins again; the other is still the same. Midnight is only a dissimulated noon, and the great Noon is the abyss of light from which we can never depart. (EI 224/IC 149)

This weakening of negation—which is also experienced at those decisive moments in the *Phenomenology of Spirit*, in history, when negation is discovered to be at a certain distance from the *Phenomenology of Spirit*, from history—will have profound consequences. Returning to a passage quoted (in part) earlier:

> [I]f we will grant that all modern humanism, the work of science, and planetary development have as their object a dissatisfaction with what is, and thus the desire to transform being—to negate it in order to derive power from it and to make of this power to negate the infinite movement of human mastery—then it will become apparent that this sort of weakness of the negative, and the way in which nothingness unmasks itself in the being that cannot be negated, lays waste at one stroke to our attempts to dominate the earth and to free ourselves from nature by giving it a meaning—that is, by denaturing it. (EI 225/IC 149)

The desire to transform being by negating it, fueled by a dissatisfaction with what is, is interrupted by the weakness of the negative. Nihilism is the impossibility of being done with the being with which one is dissatisfied and of finding a way out even in that end that is nothingness. One can never definitively go beyond.

This production of a step/not beyond is likewise traced in *Thus Spoke Zarathustra*. Zarathustra prophesies the overman as the overcoming of the nihilistic evaluations of human beings. The overman, insofar as he maintains the pure essence of will in willing nothingness, is the pure form of nihilism.

[H]is [i.e., the overman's] essential trait, the will, would make him, in his pure rigor and his harshness, the very form of nihilism for, according to Nietzsche's clear statement, *"the will would rather will nothingness than not will"* [see GdM 430/GoM 163]. The overman is he in whom nothingness makes itself will and who, free for death, maintains this pure essence of will in willing nothingness. This would be nihilism itself. (EI 222/IC 148)

At this moment, the overman, like Dasein in the act of authentic (*eigentlich*), resolute, determinate, and decided assumption of death, is "free for death" (see SZ 266/BT 311). This would be the extreme point or extreme form of nihilism. But in *Thus Spoke Zarathustra*, as in *On the Genealogy of Morals*, this step beyond is equivocal. Immediately following his announcement of the eternal return in "On the Vision and the Riddle," Zarathustra encounters a young shepherd gagging on a heavy black snake. In "The Convalescent," Zarathustra's remarks are reminiscent of this encounter: "The great disgust with man—*this* choked me and had crawled into my throat; and what the soothsayer said: 'All is the same, nothing is worth while, knowledge chokes.' A long twilight limped before me, a sadness, weary to death, drunken with death [*eine todesmüde, todestrunkene Traurigkeit*], speaking with a yawning mouth.[7] 'Eternally recurs the man of whom you are weary, the small man'" (ASZ 270/TSZ 219). Zarathustra's disgust arises, Blanchot writes, from his understanding that

> he will never definitively go beyond man's insufficiency, or that he will only be able to do so, paradoxically, by willing his return [*retour*]. But what does this return [*retour*] mean? It means what it affirms: that the extreme point of nihilism is precisely there where it reverses itself [*se renverse*], that nihilism is this very turning itself [*le retournement même*], the affirmation that, in passing from the No to the Yes, refutes nihilism, but does nothing other than affirm it, and henceforth extends it to every possible affirmation.[8] [A footnote here reads: "Hence one can conclude that nihilism identifies itself with the will to surmount it *absolutely*" (EI 225n1/IC 451n9).] (EI 225/IC 149–50)

The extreme point of nihilism is, I would suggest, the moment when death as possibility turns into death as impossibility. It is, as that which interrupts the step of the *Aufhebung*, a moment that does not appear in itself, but that merely leaves a trace of itself. It leaves a trace of itself in the production of an interminable step/not beyond, an incessant step beyond that eternally returns. The extreme point of nihilism, as reversal itself (as turning itself), leaves a trace of itself in the production or performance of a reversal, a return.

The work of Levinas, like these readings of the work of Hegel, Nietzsche, and Heidegger, contests the philosophical and religious tradition that interprets death either as a passage to nothingness or as a passage to a new way of being. The approach of death "is a relation with an instant whose exceptional character is due not to the fact that it is at the threshold of nothingness or of a rebirth, but to the fact that, in life, it is the impossibility of every possibility" (TeI 212/TaI 235). Levinas calls this moment between being and nothingness—this moment of proximity in the work of these thinkers—"dead time" (TeI 29/TaI 58).

Levinas's description of death draws upon his reading of Descartes' *Meditations*. The subject's relationship with the infinite and with the evil genius *is* its relationship with death as (im)possibility. In his description of death, Levinas writes: "Death threatens me from beyond. This unknown that frightens, the silence of the infinite spaces that terrify, comes from the other, and this alterity, precisely as absolute, strikes me in an evil design or in a judgment of justice" (TeI 210/TaI 234). This alterity strikes me in a judgment of justice (which will be considered in the next chapter) and in an evil design. Levinas also refers to this "silence" in the context of the *il y a*—"Nothing responds to us, but this silence; the voice of this silence is understood and frightens like the silence of those infinite spaces Pascal speaks of" (DEE 95/EE 58)—and in the context of the *il y a* and the evil genius—"It [i.e., silence] is the inverse of language: the interlocutor has given a sign, but has declined every interpretation; this is the silence that terrifies" (TeI 64/TaI 91).

> Death is a menace that approaches me as a mystery; its secrecy determines it—it approaches without being able to be assumed, such that the time that separates me from my death dwindles and dwindles without end, involves a sort of last interval which my consciousness cannot traverse, and where a leap will somehow be produced from death to me. The last part of the route will be crossed without me; the time of death flows upstream; the I in its projection toward the future is overturned by a movement of imminence, pure menace, which comes to me from an absolute alterity. (TeI 211/TaI 235)

Here one sees the inexorable approach of death, the not yet of death, death as the impossibility of dying.

Death as the impossibility of dying—the primordial form of the equivocality of the lived body and the physical body (TeI 212/TaI 235), of the ambiguous event of "dwelling"—is lived as physical suffering. In and through physical suffering the interval of the not yet or dead time is lived.[9] As such, suffering is ambiguous. One the one hand, the suffocating presence of physical pain leaves no room for hollowing out a safe haven. "The whole acuity of suffering lies in the impossibility of fleeing it, of being protected in oneself from oneself; it lies in being cut off from every living spring. And it is the impossibility of retreat" (TeI 215/TaI 238). "Nowhere to run ain't got nowhere to go" (Springsteen). On the other hand, at the moment one is backed up against being, one is, at the same time, at a distance from that pain. In this sense suffering, like the evil genius and the infinite, interrupts thought. It is a moment in consciousness's comprehension when consciousness finds itself at a distance from itself. "Suffering remains ambiguous: it is already the present of the pain acting on the for itself of the will, but, as consciousness, the pain is always yet to come [*toujours encore l'avenir*]. In suffering the free being ceases to be free, but, while non-free, is yet [*est encore*] free. It remains at a distance [*à distance*] from this pain by its very consciousness" (TeI 215/TaI 238). Its pain is not yet. Levinas calls this situation "patience." Echoing his earlier analysis of dwelling that is articulated by the body, Levinas writes that in patience "a disengagement within engagement is effected" (TeI 216/TaI 238) and, as such, it signifies an exposure to absolute alterity.

The interval of the not yet or dead time that marks this exposure to absolute alterity is ambiguous. This exposure not only describes a menace or persecution *by the other*, but also a responsibility *for the other*. "The will, already betrayal and alienation of itself but postponing this betrayal, on the way to death but a death ever future, exposed to death but not *immediately*, has time to be for the Other [*pour Autrui*], and thus to recover meaning [*sens*] despite death" (TeI 213/TaI 236). What is the relationship of this sense (*sens*) of responsibility *for the other* and the non-sense (*non-sens*) of menace or persecution *by the other*?

Chapter 5

Responsibility:
Rereading "On the Genealogy of Death"

Responsibility, like many words in Levinas's work, lends itself to being too easily read. It is, for Levinas, a profoundly enigmatic concept. This concept—again, like many in Levinas's work—possesses a genealogy and calls for being read accordingly. It possesses a genealogy that at a certain moment calls an initial reading into question, thereby calling for a reading that necessarily, yet impossibly, thinks together two otherwise contradictory movements. I would suggest that the genealogy of responsibility calls for being read alongside the genealogy of death traced in chapter 4, which in turn, I would further suggest, calls for it being read alongside the work of Derrida and Blanchot. Given that chapter 4 is the hinge around which this book opens and closes, the reading of responsibility alongside death undertaken in this chapter will also include a rereading of chapters 1 through 3 alongside the aporias of death and responsibility.

Derrida's *The Gift of Death* will provide initially the framework for this reading. Despite the fact that *The Gift of Death* is overtly a reading of Patočka's *Heretical Essays in the Philosophy of History* and Kierkegaard's *Fear and Trembling*, it is also, I would suggest, a supplement to Derrida's other readings of the work of Levinas.

The Gift of Death begins with a reading of "Is Technological Civilization Decadent, and Why?" one of the *Heretical Essays in the Philosophy of History* of the Czech philosopher Jan Patočka. The reading traces a genealogy of responsibility: demonic or orgiastic mystery, Platonic mystery, Christian mystery. Each conversion from one mystery to the next conserves something of what is interrupted. This logic of conservative rupture, Derrida suggests, resembles the economy of a sacrifice and sometimes reminds one of the economy of sublation (*relève*) or *Aufhebung*. Patočka employs the terms *incorporation* (*přivtělení*) and *repression* (*potlačení*) to describe this double conversion: Platonic mystery incorporates demonic or orgiastic mystery and Christian mystery represses Platonic mystery. This vocabulary indicates—if, as Derrida asks, Patočka meant to give these words the meanings that they possess in psychoanalytic discourse—that in the conversion from one mystery to another the first is not destroyed, but kept inside unconsciously, after effecting a topical displacement and a hierarchical subordination (DM 18/GD 9). This language also suggests—again, if these words were meant to be given the meanings that they possess in psychoanalytic discourse—that conversion amounts to a process of mourning, to keeping within oneself that whose death must be endured (DM 18/GD 9). Even if these words were not meant to have these meanings, nothing prevents one, Derrida suggests, from experimenting with a psychoanalytic reading, or at least a hermeneutics that takes psychoanalytic concepts corresponding to these words into account. This is especially true given that Derrida's reading concentrates on "secrecy" (or mystery), which cannot remain immune to the psychoanalytic ideas of incorporation and repression.

At various moments in Patočka's genealogy Derrida draws attention to structures in the work of Heidegger and Levinas that are "analogous" to structures in the work of Patočka. In what follows not only will I remain attentive to the analogies mentioned by Derrida, but I will also suggest others. It is important to point out, however, that I am *not* suggesting that one can reconcile the work of Patočka with the work of either Heidegger or Levinas. When Derrida suggests that a structure in Patočka's work is analogous to a structure in Heidegger's work, he prefaces his remark by writing: "without wanting to neglect the essential differences" (DM 23/GD 15). When I suggest that Derrida's reading of Patočka's *Heretical Essays in the Philosophy of History* is a supplement to Derrida's other readings of the work of Levinas, or when I suggest that there are certain analogous structures in the work of Patočka and Levinas, I (like Derrida) do it without wanting to neglect the essential differences.

What is at stake in the genealogy of the conversion from one secrecy (or mystery) to another is the gift of death. That *The Gift of Death* is a supplement to Derrida's other readings of the work of Levinas is suggested on the first page. Derrida indicates that Patočka, "[s]omewhat in the manner of Levinas," cautions against an enthusiasm for fusion with the sacred that has as its effect (and frequently its intention) absolution from responsibility (DM 11/GD 1). The first awakening to responsibility in the Platonic turn from this demonic or orgiastic mystery to the Good corresponds, for Patočka, to a conversion with respect to the apprehension of death. Philosophy comes into being as such at the moment when the soul not only assembles itself within itself in "practicing (for) death," but also is ready to receive death, "giving it to itself even," in a manner that delivers it from the body as well as from the demonic and the orgiastic (DM 44/GD 40). The famous passage from Plato's *Phaedo*, to which Patočka only obliquely refers, describes the practice of philosophy as the soul's attainment of its own freedom and responsibility in its passage to death.

> The truth rather is that the soul which is pure at departing and draws after her no bodily taint, having never voluntarily during life had connexion with the body [*ouden koinōnousa autō en tō biō hekousa einai*], which she is ever avoiding [*pheugousa*], herself gathered in herself [*synethroismenē hautēs eis heautēn*], and making such abstraction her perpetual study [*hate meletōsa aei touto*]—all this means that she has been a true disciple of philosophy [*he orthōs philosophousa*]; and therefore has in fact been always practising how to die without complaint [*kai tō onti tethnanai meletōsa rhadiōs*]. For is not such a life the practice of death [*ē ou tout' an eie meletē thanatou*]? (*Phaedo* 80e)

In "practicing (for) death" the soul separates from the body to assemble itself within itself (DM 21–22/GD 14). It is important to point out that the soul does not first exist and *then* become concerned about its death. The soul secrets itself—in the sense of the Latin *secretum* (from *secernere*), separate, distinct—in returning to itself (in both senses of assembling itself and waking itself) only in the experience of the *meletē thanatou*, the care taken with death, the "practicing (for) death" (DM 21–22/GD 13–15).

That *The Gift of Death* is a supplement to Derrida's other readings of the work of Levinas is suggested again with this passage from Plato's *Phaedo*. After drawing a parallel between Patočka and Levinas in his description of the first moment in Patočka's genealogy of responsibility, Derrida again draws attention to Levinas in this the second moment of the genealogy. Bracketed within the quotation from Plato's *Phaedo*, Derrida writes: "[W]henever Levinas refers to the *Phaedo*, as he often does in his different texts on death, he underlines this assembling of the soul upon itself as the moment when the self identifies with itself in its relation to death" (DM 22/GD 14). I would suggest that this moment in the genealogy parallels the first moment of what could be called Levinas's "genealogy of death." This moment, which reads death as the possibility of impossibility, is linked to a particular reading of Heidegger's existential analysis of death in *Being and Time*. In *The Gift of Death*, Derrida writes that the *Phaedo* names philosophy as the anticipation of death, the care involved in the "practicing (for) death," the experience of a vigil over the possibility of death as impossibility (DM 21/GD 12–13). Given the link Derrida makes between *meletē* and the sense Heidegger confers on *Sorge* in *Being and Time*, and aware of the essential differences between the two, could one read the assembling of oneself in the Platonic sense as the drawing back from inauthenticity effected in authentic being-towards-death? After noting that this concern for death, this awakening that keeps vigil over death, is another name for freedom, he adds to the link he has already made between Plato and Heidegger by noting that here again, "without wanting to neglect the essential differences," one can see in the link between the concern of the being-towards-death and freedom (that is, responsibility) a structure analogous to Dasein as described by Heidegger in *Being and Time* (DM 23/GD 15–16). The *acceptance* in and of itself (*eigentlich*) of death is the language characteristic of that reading of Heidegger's existential analysis of death that reads death as possibility.[1] It is the language of the first moment of the genealogy of death traced in chapter 4. Given the linkage drawn by Derrida, it suggests that the Platonic moment in the genealogy of responsibility is being read alongside death as possibility.

The third moment of the genealogy of responsibility, Christian mystery, announces a new apprehension of death, a new gift of death. The conversion from the Platonic mystery to the Christian mystery involves the entrance of the gift upon the scene of Patočka's genealogical drama.

> Responsible life was itself presented as a gift from something which ultimately, though it has the character of the Good, has also the traits of the inaccessible [*nepřístupného*] and forever superior to humans—the traits of the *mysterium* that always has the final word. Christianity, after all, understands the Good differently than Plato—as a self-forgetting goodness and a self-denying (not orgiastic) love. (TCU 115/TCD 106)

With the conversion, the light or sun of the Platonic Good (as the invisible source of intelligible visibility) becomes in Christianity a personal gaze (DM 89/GD 93). The gift is received from the other, the transcendent other who sees without being seen, who remains inaccessible. The dissymmetry of this gaze is identified in Christian mystery as the terrifying mystery, the *mysterium tremendum* (DM 34/GD 27). This terror does not play a role in the Platonic moment of the genealogical drama of responsibility. The terror of this secret "exceeds and precedes" the complacent relation of a subject to the Platonic Good (DM 34/GD 28). What is given in this terrifying mystery is a gift of death. The difference between Platonism and Christianity is a new apprehension of death. The difference is "the turn in the face of death and death eternal; which lives in anxiety and hope inextricably intertwined, which trembles in the knowledge of its sin and with its whole being offers itself in the sacrifice of penance" (TCU 116/TCD 108). What is given—and this represents, as will become apparent in a moment, a new apprehension of death—is a "giving goodness" that forgets itself.

Goodness is given in that the inaccessible other calls me to goodness, calls me to be good, that is, forget myself. "It subjects its receivers, giving itself to them as goodness itself but also as the law" (DM 45/GD 41). With this gift there is the emergence of a new form of responsibility, *and, at the same time*, a new apprehension of death. The experience of responsibility on the basis of the law that is given, that is, the experience of irreplaceability, is the same as the experience of irreplaceability "given" by the approach of death. "It is the same gift, the same source, one could say the same goodness and the same law" (DM 45/GD 41). It is from the experience of death as the "gift" of irreplaceable singularity that I feel called to responsibility.

Patočka's analysis is to a certain extent, Derrida notes, comparable to the existential analysis of Heidegger's *Being and Time*. According to *Being and Time*, to the extent that the self of the *Jemeinigkeit* is irreplaceable— which is given by death—it is the place in which the call (*Ruf*) is heard and in which responsibility comes on the scene (DM 49/GD 45–46).

Derrida reads the work of Heidegger alongside that moment of Patočka's genealogy of responsibility called "Christianity." This reading focuses, however, only on that moment of the genealogy of death that reads death as possibility, that is, that moment of the genealogy of death that gives irreplaceability. Irreplaceability, according to *Being and Time* is given by death. "By its very essence, death is in every case mine, in so far as it 'is' at all" (SZ 240/BT 284). This formulation follows a consideration of sacrifice. There is no gift of self, no sacrifice, Derrida writes, apart from the irreplaceability given by the approach of death. Despite the admission that Heidegger does not formulate it this way, Derrida writes that this reading does not betray Heidegger's thinking that pays, "as much as" Levinas's, incessant attention to the founding possibility of sacrifice (DM 46/GD 42). Heidegger writes: "*No one can take the Other's dying away from him* [*Keiner kann dem Anderen sein Sterben abnehmen*]. Of course someone can 'go to his death for another'. But that always means to sacrifice oneself for the Other '*in some definite affair*' (SZ 240/BT 284). While I can die for the other (by sacrificing myself for the other), I cannot, Heidegger immediately adds, die for the other (by dying in place of the other). "Such 'dying for' [*Solches Sterben für . . .*] can never signify that the Other has thus had his death taken away in even the slightest degree [*dem Anderen . . . abgenommen sei*]. Dying is something that every Dasein itself must take upon itself at the time [*Das Sterben muß jedes Dasein jeweilig selbst auf sich nehmen*]" (SZ 240/BT 284). In these sentences Derrida notes a shift from *abnehmen* to *aufnehmen* in the sense of *auf sich nehmen*. The death that cannot be taken away (*abnehmen*) must be taken upon oneself (*auf sich nehmen*). I must appropriate death, I must assume this possibility of impossibility, if I am to have access to what is irreplaceably mine (which is the condition of the possibility of sacrifice). It is not as though there is a self of the *Jemeinigkeit* that *then* comes to be a being-towards-death. It is in the authentic being-towards-death, the appropriation of death, that the self of the *Jemeinigkeit* is constituted, that its irreplaceability is produced. To this extent, Derrida's reading is not unlike his reading of the Platonic moment in Patočka's genealogy of responsibility. In a reading of Plato's *Phaedo*, Derrida points out that the soul does not first exist and *then* become concerned about its death. The soul secrets itself in returning to itself (in both senses of assembling itself and waking itself) only in the experience of the *meletē thanatou*, the care taken with death, the "practicing (for) death" (DM 21–22/GD 13–15). Aware of the essential differences between the two, Derrida seems to make a link between the assembling of oneself in the Platonic sense and the drawing back from inauthenticity effected in authentic being-towards-death. To this extent, the reading of that moment of Patočka's genealogy of responsibility called "Christianity" (at least insofar as it is limited to the link Derrida makes between the work of Patočka and the work of Heidegger) is not unlike the reading of the "Platonic" moment in the genealogy insofar as it reads death as possibility.

This reading is maintained in Derrida's consideration of the call (*Ruf*). According to *Being and Time*, to the extent that the self of the *Jemeinigkeit* is irreplaceable—which is given by death—it is the place in which the call (*Ruf*) is heard and in which responsibility comes on the scene (DM 49/GD 45–46).

Derrida's reading of the work of Heidegger alongside that moment of Patočka's genealogy of responsibility called "Christianity" is limited, however, by reading death merely as possibility. This limitation is hinted at in the text with the remark that he will need to come back to the principle involved in Levinas's objection to Heidegger in a rereading of Heidegger's analysis of death as the possibility of the impossibility of Dasein (DM 49–50/GD 46). This rereading, which I would suggest is performed in Derrida's *Aporias*, corrects the limitation of a particular reading of death in the work of Heidegger (that is, death as possibility) that prevents a comprehensive reading of it alongside that moment of Patočka's genealogy of responsibility called "Christianity" and raises the question of the proximity of the work of Heidegger and Levinas.

It already has been logically deduced that the experience of responsibility as the experience of irreplaceability is given by death (DM 45/GD 41). Derrida reads this moment of Patočka's Christianity alongside a reading of death in Heidegger that reads death as possibility. But the mortal thus deduced is one whose responsibility requires that one concern oneself not only with an objective Good that Patočka associates with Platonism, but with a goodness that is forgetful of itself, that is, a goodness that is a gift of infinite love (DM 54/GD 51). Therefore, there is a dissymmetry between the finite and responsible mortal and the goodness of the infinite gift. One is never responsible enough (and, therefore, guilty before any fault is determined) not only because one is finite, but also because of the aporetic character of responsibility. Responsibility requires two contradictory movements. "It requires one to respond as oneself and as irreplaceable singularity, to answer for what one does, says, gives; but it also requires that, being good and through goodness, one forget or efface the origin of what one gives" (DM 55/GD 51). It is on this aporetic structure in Patočka's Christianity, succinctly presented in the last two citations, that I propose to focus. I would suggest that it is only Derrida's rereading of Heidegger's analysis of death as possibility that is adequate to the aporetic structure of responsibility.[2]

Heidegger says that for Dasein (and for Dasein alone) impossibility as death is possible, that is, can appear as such and announce itself. Dasein alone is capable of this aporia. "And," Derrida adds in *Aporias*, "it is only in the act of authentic (*eigentlich*), resolute, determinate, and decided assumption by which *Dasein* would take upon itself the possibility of this impossibility that the aporia *as such* would announce itself *as such* and purely to *Dasein* as its most proper possibility, hence as the most proper essence of *Dasein*, its freedom, its ability to question, and its opening to the meaning of being" (AM 336/AD 74–75). Here Derrida asks the possible/impossible question that sets the stage for the ruinous performance of the necessary yet impossible step beyond into authenticity that is at the heart of the possibility of the existential analysis: what difference is there between the possibility of appearing as such of the possibility of an impossibility and the *im*possibility of appearing as such of the possibility of an impossibility (AM 336/AD 75)? Paralleling the first part of this possible/impossible question, Derrida writes: "According to Heidegger, it is therefore the impossibility of the 'as such' that, *as such, would be possible* to *Dasein*" (AM 336/AD 75, emphasis added to "would be possible"), would appear as such to Dasein. It is important to note that this step remains this side of ruination. It remains, as Derrida noted earlier, the act of authentic, resolute, determinate, and decided assumption by which Dasein would take upon itself the possibility of this impossibility. But then a "but" announces a change in nuance. Paralleling the second part of the possible/impossible question, Derrida writes: "But if the impossibility of the 'as such' is indeed the impossibility of the 'as such' [i.e., if the impossibility of the as such is *indeed impossible*], it [i.e., the impossibility of the as such] is *also* what cannot appear as such" (AM 336/AD 75, emphasis added), is *also* what *would not be possible* to Dasein, contrary—and is it contrary?—to what is said in the step performed just prior to the "but." "Indeed," Derrida adds, "this relation to the disappearing as such of the 'as such'—the 'as such' that

Heidegger makes the distinctive mark and the specific ability of *Dasein* [i.e.,
the authentic, resolute, determinate, and decided assumption of the possibility
of the impossibility of death]—is also the characteristic common *both* to the
inauthentic *and* to the authentic forms of the existence of *Dasein*" (AM
336/AD 75). The fact that the impossibility that *would be possible* to Dasein
(in authentic existence) cannot appear as such, that is, *would not be possible*
to Dasein (even in authentic existence) erases the distinction between the
inauthentic (in which impossibility as death does *not* appear as such, is
evaded) and the authentic (in which impossibility as death *supposedly* can
appear). Here one sees the ruination of the step that would complete the existential analysis *in the performance of the step itself.* Here one sees the
unworking of the work.

With this reading in *Aporias*, Derrida shows how what is at the very
heart of the possibility of the existential analysis of death as possibility of the
impossibility of the Dasein can be turned against the very possibility of the
existential analysis, depending on the way one reads the expression "the possibility of impossibility" (AM 336–37/AD 76–77). This is the context of Derrida's remark that "[w]hen Blanchot constantly repeats—and it is a long complaint and not a triumph of life—the impossible dying, the impossibility, alas,
of dying, he says at once the same thing and something completely different
from Heidegger" (AM 337/AD 77). Turning what is at the very heart of the
possibility of the existential analysis of death, that is, the appropriation of
death, against the very possibility of the existential analysis, Derrida writes:
"If death, the most proper possibility of *Dasein*, is the possibility of its impossibility, death becomes the most improper possibility and the most ex-propriating, the most inauthenticating one" (AM 337/AD 77). This passage, along
with the previous passage that raises the question of the proximity of the work
of Heidegger and Blanchot, echoes "the radical reversal" referred to by Blanchot in *The Space of Literature.*

> Death, then, would not be "the possibility absolutely proper to man,"
> my own death, that unique event which answers Rilke's prayer: "O
> Lord, grant to each his own death," but on the contrary, that which never
> happens to me, so that never do I die, but rather "they die." Men die
> always other than themselves, at the level of the neutrality and the
> impersonality of the eternal They.
>
> The characteristics of this reversal can only be recalled briefly
> here.
>
> *They die*: this is not a reassuring formula designed to put off the
> fearsomemoment. *They die*: he who dies is anonymous, and anonymity
> is the guise in which the ungraspable, the unlimited, the unsituated is
> most dangerously affirmed among us. (EL 327/SL 241)

This "radical reversal"—death as possibility turning into death as impossibility—parallels the two contradictory movements of responsibility characteristic, according to Derrida's reading, of Patočka's Christianity. Only it—and not simply death as possibility—is adequate to the aporetic structure of responsibility. Responsibility requires, as was mentioned earlier, that one respond as irreplaceable singularity *and*, paradoxically, that one forget or efface the origin of what one gives (DM 55/GD 51). Only the aporia of death—that moment when death as possibility turns into death as impossibility—is adequate to the aporia of responsibility, insofar as death as possibility gives irreplaceable singularity and death as impossibility gives the ex-propriation, the anonymity, that is a forgetting or effacement of oneself.

This reading of death is, I would suggest, operative (though not explicitly) in Blanchot's reading of responsibility in the work of Levinas. In *The Writing of the Disaster*, Blanchot shows responsibility's aporetic structure in a fragment that calls for being quoted at length:

> Responsible: this word generally qualifies—in a prosaic, bourgeois manner—a mature, lucid, conscientious man, who acts with circumspection, who takes into account all elements of a given situation, calculates and decides. The word "responsible" qualifies the successful man of action. But now responsibility—my responsibility for the other, for everyone, without reciprocity—is displaced. No longer does it belong to consciousness; it is not an activating thought process put into practice, nor is it even a duty that would impose itself from without and from within. *My* responsibility for the Other [*Autrui*] presupposes an overturning such that it can only be marked by a change in the status of "me," a change in time and perhaps in language. Responsibility, which withdraws me from my order—perhaps from all orders and from order itself—responsibility, which separates me from myself (from the "me" that is mastery and power, from the free, speaking subject) and reveals the other [*autre*] *in place* of me, requires that I answer for absence, for passivity. It requires, that is to say, that I answer for the impossibility of being responsible—to which it has always already consigned me by holding me accountable and also discounting me altogether. (ED 45–46/WD 25)

Responsibility requires that I respond, that I answer for what I do, say, and give, as irreplaceable singularity, and it requires that I am exposed to ex-propriation, to anonymity, that I forget or efface myself, that I be (in Levinas's words) nothing but "for the Other." In other words, responsibility requires—using words of Blanchot that echo Heidegger's analysis of death as possibility of the impossibility of Dasein—that I answer for the impossibility of being responsible, which makes me always already guilty or irresponsible. The more I am responsible, the more irresponsible I am, because (on the one hand) responsibility holds me accountable, and (on the other hand) responsibility discounts me (insofar as it requires that I be selfless). Only death as possibility turning into death as impossibility is adequate to this aporia of responsibility.

This reading of death—death as possibility turning into death as impossibility—not only corrects Derrida's limited reading of the work of Heidegger alongside that moment of Patočka's genealogy of responsibility called "Christianity" (a limited reading in that it focuses only on that moment of the genealogy of death that reads death as possibility), but also calls for being read alongside the work of Levinas (as was hinted at in the preceding paragraph). It is important to point out that in the preceding paragraphs—where I suggest that only the moment when death as possibility turns into death as impossibility is adequate to the aporetic structure of responsibility—I am *not* suggesting that the work of Patočka, Heidegger, Levinas, and Blanchot can be reconciled. The question of the proximity of these thinkers is raised only with respect to the moment when death as possibility turns into death as impossibility. At this moment, if only for a moment, one can think together the work of Levinas and other thinkers. This is not done out of ignorance of the essential differences between the thinkers. It is not done out of ignorance of the different horizons of thought from which their works emerge. It is done with an attentiveness to those decisive moments in their work when work is discovered to be at a certain distance from that work.

That the aporia of responsibility must be read alongside the aporia of death is attested to at length in the work of Levinas. This attestation also supports the suggestion made earlier that Derrida's *The Gift of Death* is a supplement to his other readings of the work of Levinas. In *Totality and Infinity* Levinas writes: "Death threatens me from beyond. This unknown that frightens, the silence of the infinite spaces that terrify, comes from the other, and this alterity, precisely as absolute, strikes me in an evil design or in a judgment of justice" (TeI 210/TaI 234). The absolute alterity of death strikes me in an evil design or in a judgment of justice, which, as will become apparent, are tightly woven together. The judgment of justice, coming from the absolute alterity of the other, is often referred to by Levinas as a "judgment of God," that is, a judgment pronounced by the infinite.

Levinas situates this judgment of God or justice and the accompanying summons to absolute responsibility within the context of the aporia of death. In a passage that is echoed in Derrida's *The Gift of Death*, Levinas writes that the judgment of God or justice

> is pronounced upon me in the measure that it summons me to respond. [. . .] The summons exalts the singularity precisely because it

is addressed to an infinite responsibility. *The infinity of responsibility denotes not its actual immensity, but a responsibility increasing in the measure that it is assumed*; duties become greater in the measure that they are accomplished. The better I accomplish my duty the fewer rights I have; the more I am just the more guilty I am. The I [. . .] is confirmed in its singularity by purging itself of [. . .] gravitation, purges itself interminably, and is confirmed precisely in this incessant effort to purge itself. This is termed goodness. (TeI 222/TaI 244–45)

The deepening of my responsibility in the judgment of God or justice that is borne upon me calls for being read alongside the aporia of death.

The deepening of my responsibility in the judgment that is borne upon me is not of the order of universalization: beyond the justice of universal laws, the I enters under judgment by the fact of being good. Goodness consists in taking up a position in being such that the Other counts more than myself. Goodness thus involves the possibility for the I that is exposed to the alienation of its powers by death to not be for death. (TeI 225/TaI 247)

Responsibility requires that I respond as irreplaceable singularity, and it requires that I purge myself interminably, that I be exposed to the alienation of my powers. In other words, responsibility requires—using words of Blanchot that echo Heidegger's analysis of death as possibility of the impossibility of Dasein—that I answer for the impossibility of being responsible, which makes me always already guilty or irresponsible. The more I am responsible, the more irresponsible I am. This aporia of responsibility calls for being read alongside the aporia of death. It is important to note that while readings of Heidegger tend to focus on the singularizing aspect of death, Levinas tends to focus on the alienating aspect of death. The two must necessarily, yet impossibly, be read together.

Only the aporia of death—that moment when death as possibility turns into death as impossibility—is adequate to the aporia of responsibility, insofar as death as possibility gives irreplaceable singularity and death as impossibility gives the ex-propriation that is the exposure of the I to the alienation of its powers. *I* am never up to the task. The work at hand is beyond me. The more I am responsible (that is, the more I authentically, resolutely, determinately, and decidedly assume death, which gives absolute irreplaceable singularity), the more irresponsible I am (that is, the more I am ex-propriated or "inauthentic," exposed to anonymity, immersed in the "they," an indistinguishable one among many, unable to respond as irreplaceable singularity). It is important to note that this moment of ex-propriation, anonymity, or "inauthenticity," in responsibility is *not* a reassuring conclusion that absolves one of the terrifying work of responsibility. It is *not*—as Blanchot notes, though with respect to death (the most proper possibility of Dasein) becoming the most improper possibility and the most ex-propriating, inauthenticating possibility—"a reassuring formula designed to put off the fearsome," but rather the dangerous affirmation of "the ungraspable, the unlimited, the unsituated" among us (EL 327/SL 241).

The judgment of God or justice that indicts my arbitrary freedom does not, therefore, simply "seal my [as well as the other's] pure and simple entry into the universal order" (TeI 222/TaI 245), that is, an order impersonally and implacably governed by a universal principle of justice, as is the case in the "judgment of history." In the judgment of God or justice that "summons me to respond," that is "addressed to an infinite responsibility" (TeI 222/TaI 244), one is summoned (given the aporetic character of responsibility) to go beyond justice understood as a universal principle. That is, there is never a point at which I would satisfy the law, find a resting place in a good conscience. There is no limit to my responsibility. I am summoned to do that which is impossible for me to do. In the judgment of God or justice that—like the movement of critique (or doubt)—indicts the arbitrary freedom of comprehension's free exercise,

> justice does not include me in the equilibrium of its universality; justice summons me to go beyond the straight line of justice, and henceforth nothing can mark the end of this march; behind the straight line of the law the land of goodness extends infinite and unexplored, necessitating all the resources of a singular presence. I am therefore necessary for justice,[3] as responsible beyond every limit fixed by an objective law. The I is a privilege and an election. The sole possibility in being of going beyond the straight line of the law, that is, of finding a place lying beyond the universal, is to be I. (TeI 223/TaI 245)

To be I is to be unable to be absolved of responsibility, unable to shirk one's responsibility. "The accomplishing of the I qua I and morality constitute one sole and same process in being: morality comes to birth not in equality [i.e., not in the equilibrium of the universal order of justice], but in the fact that infinite exigencies, that of serving the poor, the stranger, the widow, and the orphan, converge at one point of the universe" (TeI 223/TaI 245). Just as one's singularity is confirmed in death, one's singularity is confirmed in objective judgment. But this confirmation is, at the same time (according to the logic of the aporias of death and responsibility), an ex-propriation, a forgetting or effacement of oneself, a being nothing but "for the Other." Levinas can write that "[t]he person is [. . .] confirmed in objective judgment and no longer reduced to his place within a totality" (TeI 223–24/TaI 246) because, as he wrote earlier, the judgment of "justice does not include me in the equilibrium of its universality; justice summons me to go beyond the straight line of justice, and henceforth nothing can mark the end of this march" (TeI 223/TaI 245). There is an "incessant overflowing of duty accomplished, by ever broader responsibilities" (TeI 223/TaI 246). Therefore, this confirmation of the singularity of the I in objective judgment, as in death, "does not consist in flattering his subjective tendencies and consoling him for his death, but in existing for the Other [*pour autrui*], that is, in being called in question and in dreading murder more than death—a *salto mortale* whose perilous space is opened forth and measured already by patience (and this is the meaning [*sens*] of suffering), but which the singular being par excellence—an I—can alone accomplish" (TeI 224/TaI 246). *Salto mortale*, a phrase Levinas associates with Kierkegaard (DL 191–92/DF 144), is commonly translated into English as "leap of faith." The more literal translation of "deadly leap" would perhaps be more appropriate in this particular context, for the perilous space of this *salto mortale* refers, I would suggest, to the aporia of death—death as possibility turning into death as impossibility—and its effect on the work of absolute responsibility. It refers to a leap or step beyond that is, *at the same time*, not beyond. It refers to the ruination of the step that is the work of absolute responsibility *in the performance of the step itself*, that is, to the unworking of the work of absolute responsibility.

Reading death alongside responsibility calls the linearity of Levinas's work into question. The analysis of death in *Totality and Infinity* (TeI 208–13/TaI 232–36, which echoes Levinas's reading of the evil genius in Descartes' *Meditations*; TeI 62–66/TaI 90–94) opens up (like the reading of the evil genius) a relationship with the other, albeit a relationship whose intentionality is one of menace or persecution. It may seem, given the narrative of *Totality and Infinity* (and the suggestions of many readers of Levinas), that the analysis of the aporia of death that opens a relationship whose intentionality is one of menace or persecution *by the other* gives way to (and, according to some readings, is a necessary step on the way to) the aporia of death that opens up a relationship whose intentionality is one of responsibility *for the other*. Or said otherwise, it may seem that Levinas rather unambiguously steps beyond menace or persecution by the other to a responsibility for the other. But this step is, as Paul Davies points out, highly problematic.[4] The moment of ex-propriation in death that makes one vulnerable to the non-sense of the *il y a* never can be rigorously separated from the sense of responsibility.

The non-sense of the *il y a* is not prevalent in Levinas's discussion of justice in *Totality and Infinity*. *Otherwise than Being* is more attentive to the inevitable confusion of the by-the-other (the non-sense of the *il y a*; AE 208/OB 163) and the for-the-other (the sense of responsibility).

> Of itself saying is the sense [*sens*] of patience and pain. In saying suf-
> fering signifies in the form of *giving*, even if the price of signification
> is that the subject run the risk [*courait le risque*] of suffering without
> reason. If the subject did not run this risk [*ne courait pas ce risque*],
> pain would lose its very painfulness. Signification, as the one-for-the-
> other in passivity, where the other is not assumed by the one, presup-
> poses the possibility of pure non-sense invading and threatening signi-
> fication. Without this folly at the confines of reason, the one would take
> hold of itself, and, in the heart of its passion, recommence essence. How
> the adversity of pain is ambiguous! The for-the-other (or sense) turns
> into by-the-other [*Le pour-l'autre (ou le sens) va jusqu'au par-l'autre*],
> into suffering by a thorn burning the flesh, but *for nothing* [*pour rien*].
> It is only in this way that the *for-the-other* [*pour-l'autre*], the passivity
> more passive still than any passivity, the emphasis of sense [*sens*], is
> kept from being *for-oneself* [*pour-soi*]. (AE 64–5/OB 50)

An intentionality of menace or persecution lies at the heart of the suffering
characteristic of the judgment of God or justice, the command or prescription
of goodness. There is a "by-the-other" at the heart of the "for-the-other." The
absurdity of the *il y a* is a *modality* of the for-the-other (AE 208–9/OB 164).
This prevents the suffering from being a *virtuous* suffering, a self-edifying
suffering. Such a self-edifying suffering would be a suffering that would no
longer be (that would be blind to) the suffering of the aporia of responsibility
that involves irresponsibility, guilt. The aporia of responsibility would be
stilled. The fact that the demonic is a modality of infinite goodness is what
makes (true) responsibility possible. With this self-edifying suffering, an
ethics of good conscience re-installs itself, that is, rather than being for-the-
other, one would be for-oneself.

In is important to note that despite the fact that being responsible is
always already impossible, that is, is always already interrupted by the irresponsible, responsibility remains. Said otherwise, the impossibility of being
responsible does not absolve one of responsibility. In fact, it increases it infinitely. It is an impossible responsibility that never ends, is incessantly culpa-
ble, and is never absolved

If irresponsibility (the demonic or non-sense) interrupts responsibility,
then why does Levinas say that in absolute responsibility there is the "possibility," the "risk," the "threat," of irresponsibility, which makes it sound like a mere
possibility of the subject, something the subject could avoid if it were prudent?
For example, in *Otherwise than Being*, Levinas writes: "Signification, as the one-
for-the-other in passivity, where the other is not assumed by the one, presupposes
the *possibility* of pure non-sense invading and threatening signification" (AE
64/OB 50, emphasis added). Why not write "presupposes pure non-sense" or

even "presupposes the necessity of pure non-sense"? Perhaps the language is employed to avoid the risk of these formulations being taken as a theodicy. If one removes the language of "possibility"/"risk"/"threat," then one risks ending up with a formulation that suggests that responsibility *requires* an actual, empirical event of evil. The existence of evil would, therefore, be justified as necessary for responsibility. There is no textual evidence for this reading.

In fact, Levinas vigorously puts his work at a distance from theodicy. Levinas addresses the question of theodicy in, among other works, "Transcendence and Evil." The work is ostensibly a reading of Philippe Nemo's *Job et l'excès du Mal*. Levinas divides his reading into three moments: evil as excess, evil as intention, and evil as the hatred of evil. I will concentrate primarily on the third moment where the question of evil's proximity to good is raised. Levinas sums up the third and last moment—evil as the hatred of evil—as follows: "[E]vil strikes me in my horror of evil, and thus reveals— or is already—my association with the Good. The excess of evil by which it is a surplus in the world is also our impossibility of accepting it. The experience of evil would then be also our waiting on the good—the love of God" (TM 203/TE 183). This "movement leading from the 'horror of evil' to the discovery of the Good [. . .] completes in a theophany the transcendence opened in the totality of the world by the concrete 'content' of evil" (TM 204/TE 184). This passage raises the question of theodicy insofar as it could be read as suggesting that the discovery of the Good *requires* evil. The existence of evil would, therefore, be justified as a necessary prelude to the discovery of the Good. But Levinas insists that in this reversal of evil and of the horror of evil into an expectation of the Good there can be "no question of a passage from Evil to the Good through the attraction of contraries" for "that would make but one more theodicy" (TM 203/TE 183). Theodicy, according to Levinas, seeks the meaning of the scandal of suffering. With this meaning, Levinas writes in "Useless Suffering," "[p]ain is henceforth meaningful, subordinated in one way or another to the metaphysical finality envisaged by faith or by a belief in progress. These beliefs are presupposed by theodicy! Such is the grand idea necessary to the inner peace of souls in our distressed world. It is called upon to make sufferings here below comprehensible" (SI 333–34/US 160). Levinas acknowledges that Nemo himself is likewise sensitive to this problem when he asks: "Does not the philosophical contribution of all this Biblical exegesis consist in making it *possible* to go as it were beyond the reciprocal appeal of terms that negate one another, beyond dialectics?" (TM 203/TE 183, emphasis added). This is made possible not only because evil, as Nemo considered it in the first two moments of the book, is not any kind of negation, but also because Nemo is sensitive to Nietzsche's warning against the spirit of *ressentiment*, that is, a good that would signify only a repayment for evil or a vengeance. With this in mind Nemo describes the expectation of the Good as a thought that would think more than it thinks. This formulation is not unlike the one used by Levinas to describe the idea of infinity in his reading of Descartes' *Meditations*. The soul, torn up from the world and awakened to itself by evil, the soul beyond satisfaction and recompense, "expects an awaited that infinitely surpasses expectancy" (TM 204/TE 183–84). But despite Levinas's praise for this "very profound" formulation that makes it possible to go beyond the reciprocal appeal of contrary terms that negate one another, beyond dialectics, he asks: "Does it [i.e., the movement leading from the horror of evil to the discovery of the Good in Nemo's book] not lead to but the opposite of evil, and to a goodness of simple pleasure, however great it be?" (TM 204/TE 184). That is, does it not lead, however superlative or excessive the good may be, to a goodness that merely compensates for the evil, to a play of good and evil?

The notion of "play" designates, for Nemo, the relation of the soul with God. However, "play" cannot, according to Levinas, be deduced from the disproportion between expectation and the expected, that is, the disproportion between God and the thought that thinks God. Moreover if play is deduced from the disproportion between God and the thought that thinks God then one risks, according to Levinas, reinscribing this "very profound" formulation within a theodicy where the expectation of the Good would be reduced to the dialectical play of good and evil (understood as contraries) "in which the wholly-otherness of God [would no longer be expected but rather] would become visible" (TM 203/TE 183). To illustrate this point Levinas quotes the following passage from *Job et l'excès du Mal*: "The excess of beatitude alone will answer to the excess of evil" (TM 204/TE 184). Levinas suggests that Nemo uses two different senses of "excess" in this passage in order to maintain the privileged signification of evil around which his whole book is constructed. "The excess of evil does not mean an excessive evil, whereas the excess of beatitude remains a superlative notion. For if it were necessary to *already* see in beatitude, as such, an excess, evil would *not* have had the privileged signification about which Nemo's whole book is constructed" (TM 204/TE 184, emphasis added). But according to Levinas, it *is* necessary to *already* see in beatitude, as such, an excess. There is always already *also* an excess of good as well as an excess of evil.

This prompts Levinas to propose, in the form of a question, an alternative understanding of the movement leading from the horror of evil to the discovery of the Good that does *not* lead to the opposite of evil, to a goodness of simple pleasure. "Does not the Good that is awaited in this 'awaiting which aims at infinitely more than this awaited' maintain a relationship *less remote* with the evil which suggests it, while differing from it with a difference *more different* than opposition?" (TM 204–5/TE 184, emphasis added). And while both Nemo and Levinas recognize a disproportion between expectation and the expected, Levinas has certain reservations about designating it with the notion of "play." He will choose instead to designate it with the notions of command and prescription.

Levinas hints at this alternative designation of the disproportionate relationship between expectation and the expected when he raises "the problem of the relationship between the suffering of the self and the suffering which a self can experience over the suffering of the other man" (TM 205/TE 184)[5]— a problem which never appears on the foreground of Nemo's commentary on the Book of Job. Is there not a question of this problematical relationship, Levinas asks, in the "Where were you when I founded the earth?" of Job 38:4?

This passage, at the beginning of the discourse attributed to God, "reminds Job of his absence at the hour of creation" (TM 205/TE 184). But how is one to understand this absence? This passage has been understood commonly as an almost satirical retort to the impudence of Job—Where were *you*?[6] But, Levinas asks, does this passage "*only* set forth a theodicy in which the economy of a harmonious and wisely arranged whole harbors evil only for a look limited to a part of this whole" (TM 205/TE 184, emphasis added)? That is, does the suffering of the self as a self exposed to evil merely take hope in and await the ultimate good (understood as the contrary of evil) that lies beyond its limited look? Rather than the traditional reading of this passage— "Where were *you*?"—Levinas reads, "Where *were* you?" and asks: "Might one not understand in this 'Where were you?' a denunciation of being wanting, which can have meaning only if the humanity of man is fraternally solidary with creation, that is, is responsible for what was neither one's self nor one's work, and if this solidarity and this responsibility for everything and for all, which cannot occur without pain, is the spirit itself?" (TM 205/TE 184). This sounds similar to a passage in *The Writing of the Disaster* where, echoing Heidegger's analysis of death as possibility of the impossibility of Dasein, Blanchot writes that responsibility requires that I answer for the impossibility of being responsible (ED 46/WD 25), which makes me always already guilty. This reading, which sets forth a theophany rather than a theodicy, denounces a look limited to a part of a harmonious and wisely arranged whole. It even denounces a look that is, according to Levinas, delimited by Nemo—a look that, having been torn out of the world by evil, merely waits on the opposite of evil, the goodness of simple pleasure. The theophany set forth in this reading differs, therefore, from the theophany that Levinas believes Nemo sets forth—a theophany that risks being reduced to "one more theodicy" (TM 203/TE 183), to a mere "play" of contraries within a totalized economy.

Levinas also invokes the Book of Job in "Useless Suffering" in showing that while theodicy is justified by a certain reading of the Bible, "another reading of it [i.e., the Bible] is possible" (SI 337n7/US 167n8). The Book of Job, according to Levinas, "attests at once to Job's faithfulness to God (2:10)

and to ethics (27:5 and 6), despite his sufferings without reason, and his opposition to the theodicy of his friends" (SI 337n7/US 167n8). His refusal of
theodicy is preferred by God to those friends who "would make God innocent
before the suffering of the just" (SI 337n7/US 167n8; see Job 42:7). This,
Levinas continues, is a little like Kant's reading of the Book of Job in "On the
Failure of all the Philosophical Attempts at a Theodicy." Kant finds the following allegorically expressed in the Book of Job: faith arises only in the person who, in the conviction of ignorance with respect to the inscrutable ways
of God, does *not* renounce his/her moral integrity. "In this state of mind,"
Kant writes and Levinas quotes, "Job has proven that he did not found his
morality on faith, but his faith on morality; in which case faith, however weak
it may be, is nonetheless one of a pure and authentic kind, a kind which does
not found a religion of solicited favours, but a well conducted life" (SI
337n7/US 167n8).

The "suffering of the self" as a self exposed to evil always already
involves "the suffering which a self can experience over the suffering of the
other man." In fact, according to Levinas in "Transcendence and Evil," a "suffering of the self" that does not already involve the "suffering which a self can
experience over the suffering of the other man" never truly "expects an awaited
that infinitely surpasses expectancy," never truly expects a good that would not
signify a repayment for evil or a vengeance, a good beyond recompense.

The pain of the transgressive responsibility brought out in Levinas's
reading of the Book of Job in "Transcendence and Evil" circumvents a reading of the good inherent in the Nietzschean idea of *ressentiment*. It marks the
"relationship" of "the suffering of the self [non-sense] and the suffering which
a self can experience over the suffering of the other man [sense]."

Levinas elaborates on the ambiguity of this disturbing affliction called
"pain" in the following passage: "That in the evil that pursues me the evil suf-
fered by the other man afflicts me, that it touches me, as though [*comme si*]
from the first the other was calling to me, putting into question my resting on
myself and my *conatus essendi*, as though [*comme si*] before lamenting over
my evil here below, I had to answer for the other—is not this a breakthrough
of the Good in the 'intention' of which I am in my woe so exclusively aimed
at?" (TM 206/TE 185). The phrase *as though* (*comme si*) plays a key role in
Levinas's reading of Descartes' *Meditations*. In *Totality and Infinity*, Levinas
writes: "The cause of being [i.e., God] is thought or known by its effect [i.e.,
the *cogito*] *as though* [*comme si*] it were posterior to its effect" (TeI 25/TaI
54). The phrase *as though* articulates a double origin. Specifically, with
respect to Levinas's reading of Descartes' *Meditations*, it articulates the ambiguity of the priority of the *cogito* and the infinite. In the passage in question
the "as though" (*comme si*) articulates, I would suggest, the ambiguity of the
priority of the suffering of the self and the suffering which a self can experi-

ence over the suffering of the other man. Here there is a theophany, here there is a breakthrough of a Good that does not please, but commands.

A question arises: Given the structure of "Transcendence and Evil," is Levinas vulnerable to a similar criticism that he levels against Nemo? That is, does the Good have a privileged signification about which Levinas's whole work is constructed (see TM 204/TE 184)? Levinas frequently constructs a linear narrative that seems to step from the *il y a* (non-sense, the demonic) to the alterity of the other (sense). This step is, however, as was shown earlier, highly problematic. Despite the fact that "Transcendence and Evil" is constructed in similar fashion, what appears to be an unambiguous linear narrative is arguably tempered by the fact that Levinas is so careful to stress the ambiguity of the priority of evil and the Good, by the fact that he is careful to put his work at a distance from theodicy. Perhaps the construction of "Transcendence and Evil" is merely a vestige of earlier linear narratives (or perhaps a construction dictated by the structure of Nemo's *Job et l'excès du Mal*). In any case, it is important to keep in mind that despite the overt structure of "Transcendence and Evil," the Good does *not* have the last word. One must never remain blind to the fact that if one takes seriously not only Levinas's words (for example, in the reversal of evil and of the horror of evil into an expectation of the Good "there can here be no question of a passage from Evil to the Good through the attraction of contraries" for "that would make but one more theodicy"), but also the logic of his remarks, then the Good is always already compromised by the demonic.

The wickedness of God that persecutes is a modality of the goodness of God that commands. Echoing descriptions in *Totality and Infinity* of the evil genius in Descartes' *Meditations* and death, Levinas writes in "Transcendence and Evil" of an "intention" discovered in evil: "[E]vil reaches me as though [*comme si*] it sought me out; evil strikes me as though [*comme si*] there were an aim behind the ill lot that pursues me, as though [*comme si*] someone were set against me, as though [*comme si*] there were malice, as though [*comme si*] there were someone" (TM 200/TE 181). The ambiguity literally turns on the "as though" (*comme si*). Consider the following passages from *Totality and Infinity*, the first of which occurs in the context of a reading of the evil genius and the second of which occurs in the context of a reading of death:

> It is as though [*Comme si*] in this silent and indecisive apparition a lie were perpetuated, as though [*comme si*] the danger of error arose from an imposture, as though [*comme si*] the silence were but the modality of an utterance. (TeI 64/TaI 91)

> In the being for death of fear I am not faced with nothingness, but faced with what is *against me*, as though [*comme si*] murder, rather than being

one of the occasions of dying, were inseparable from the essence of death, as though [*comme si*] the approach of death remained one of the modalities of the relation with the Other. (TeI 210–11/TaI 234)

As mentioned earlier, the phrase *as though* (*comme si*) plays a key role in Levinas's reading of Descartes' *Meditations*. It articulates the ambiguity of the priority of the *cogito* and the infinite. In the passage in question the "as though" (*comme si*) articulates, I would suggest, the ambiguity the suffering self closed in on itself and, at the same time, exposed to the transcendence of the other. Evil awakens the ego to the you of God (TM 200/TE 181). With the intention discovered in evil, one is faced with "the somber paradox of the wickedness of God" (TM 201/TE 182). In the death (which is lived as suffering; TM 196/TE 179) that singularizes me, there is an "intentionality" of transcendence (TM 198/TE 180), but it is a malicious God, an evil genius. "God does evil to me to tear me out of the world, as unique and ex-ceptional" (TM 201/TE 182). The following serves as an epigraph to Levinas's "Transcendence and Evil": "I make peace, and create evil: I the Lord do all these things" (Isaiah 45:7).

This consideration of the role of God in a reading of death/responsibility brings one back to Derrida's reading of Patočka's Christianity in *The Gift of Death*. Recall that reading death as possibility turning into death as impossibility corrects Derrida's limited reading of the work of Heidegger alongside that moment of Patočka's genealogy of responsibility called "Christianity" (a limited reading in that it focuses only on that moment of the genealogy of death that reads death as possibility). This reading of death, when read alongside Patočka's Christianity, also opens up new ways of reading the "heretical and hyperbolic form" of Christianity (if, in fact, it does involve Christianity) in the work of Patočka (DM 52/GD 49), and thereby raises the question of the proximity of Heidegger's and Levinas's work and Patočka's Christianity.

Patočka refers, with respect to Christianity, to a supreme being who rouses me to the responsibility it gives me by giving a new apprehension of death (DM 39/GD 33).

It is not the orgiastic—that remains not only subordinated but, in certain respects, suppressed to the limit—yet it is still a *mysterium tremendum*. *Tremendum*, for responsibility is now vested not in a humanly comprehensible essence of goodness and unity but, rather, in an inscrutable relation to the absolute highest being in whose hands we are not externally, but internally. (TCU 115/TCD 106)

The definition of God as a supreme being is an onto-theological proposition that Heidegger rejects. The call (*Ruf*)—the basis of Dasein's experience of

being-responsible or being-guilty (*Schuldigsein*)—does not imply any relation to a supreme being who could be taken as the origin of the voice. Yet
Patočka, as Derrida notes, not only seems to contradict Heidegger, but he also
seems to contradict himself. At one point he writes that Nietzsche's description of Christianity as the Platonism of the people was correct because "the
Christian God took over the transcendence of the onto-theological conception
as a matter of course," whereas at another point he writes that there is "a fundamental, profound difference" between Christianity and onto-theology (TCU
116/TCD 107). To avoid this self-contradiction Patočka needs to keep his reference to a supreme being distinct from all onto-theological meaning in the
sense that Heidegger gave to it. This is without a doubt, Derrida adds, an
implicit project of Patočka's work (DM 39/GD 33).

Patočka's work is, as was mentioned earlier, a "heretical and hyperbolic
form" of Christianity (if, in fact, it does involve Christianity). Derrida points
out that "Patočka speaks and thinks in the places where Christianity has not
yet thought or spoken of what it should have been and is not yet" (DM 52/GD
49). What produces the Christian themes considered by Patočka is, according
to Derrida, a logic that ultimately has no need of the event of a revelation or
the revelation of an event. This logic needs to think the *possibility* of the event
of a revelation or the revelation of an event, but not the event itself (DM
52/GD 49). The possibility of the Christian event—that is, the gift of infinite
love (the Good as goodness that forgets itself) linked to death—can be logically deduced through the aporias of death and responsibility, though Derrida,
arguably, considers only one of the two moments in the genealogy of death
necessary in a logical deduction of Patočka's Christian responsibility. Derrida
suggests a list of philosophers, which includes Heidegger and Levinas, that
belong to a tradition "that consists of proposing a nondogmatic doublet of
dogma, a philosophical and metaphysical doublet, in any case a *thinking* that
'repeats' [«*répète*»] the possibility of religion without religion" (DM 53/GD
49). But this repetition contaminates the purity of the nondogmatic doublet of
dogma. In the wake of his rereading of Heidegger's analysis of death as possibility of the impossibility of Dasein, Derrida writes in *Aporias* that since the
contaminating contraband of Christian onto-theology remains irreducible, it
already insinuates itself through the very idiom of the existential analysis of
death (AM 338/AD 79). Therefore, he continues, "[d]espite all the distance
taken from anthropo-theology, indeed, from Christian onto-theology, the
analysis of death in *Being and Time* nonetheless repeats [*répète*] all the essential motifs of such onto-theology, a repetition [*répétition*] that bores into its
originarity right down to its ontological foundation" (AM 338/AD 80). This
passage shows that the repetition does not leave the originarity of the Heideggerian analysis unsullied. This passage marks an interruption effected in
Derrida's rereading of Heidegger's analysis of death. The interruption of the

boundary between the authentic and the inauthentic effected in Derrida's rereading effects an interruption of the originarity of the Heideggerian analysis. The fact that this repetition contaminates the purity of the nondogmatic doublet of dogma, the philosophical and metaphysical doublet, is likewise evident in *The Gift of Death*. Immediately after writing that "[e]verything *comes to pass* as though only the analysis of the concept of responsibility [as it is given by death] were ultimately capable of producing Christianity, or more precisely the possibility of Christianity," Derrida adds: "One might as well conclude, conversely, that this concept of responsibility is Christian through and through and is produced by the event of Christianity" (DM 53/GD 50). There is, in a sense, a double origin at work here. There is no choice to be made here between a logical and philosophical deduction of religious themes, that is, one that is not related to a revelatory event, and the reference to a revelatory event. "One implies the other" (DM 53/GD 50). In *Aporias*, Derrida writes: "Considering what we just have seen considering borders, demarcations, and limits, the only characteristic that we can stress here is that of an irreducibly double inclusion: the including and the included [the existential analysis of death and the Judeo-Christiano-Islamic experience of death, though not necessarily respectively] regularly exchange places in this strange topography of edges" (AM 338/AD 80).[7]

Not only is one pole of this double origin—the "nondogmatic doublet of dogma," that is, the logical deduction of responsibility through the experience of irreplaceability given in the approach of death (which, I have suggested, must be supplemented with a reading of death as impossibility)—contaminated by the reference to a revelatory event, but it likewise contaminates the purity of the dogma associated with the revelatory event, calling for a rereading of Christianity and opening a space for Patočka's "heretical and hyperbolic form" of Christianity (if, in fact, it does involve Christianity). In the conversion from Platonism to Christianity the Good is no longer a transcendental objective, but the relation to the other. It is "an experience of personal goodness and a movement of intention" (DM 54/GD 50). This goodness is a goodness that forgets itself, and this movement is a movement of the gift that renounces itself, that is, a movement of infinite love. "Only infinite love," Derrida writes, "can renounce itself and, in order to *become finite*, become incarnated in order to love the other, to love the other as a finite other" (DM 54/GD 51). Patočka's reading of Christianity involves, therefore, a double effacement or renunciation. It has already been noted that goodness is given in that the inaccessible other calls me to goodness, calls me to be good, that is, forget myself. "It subjects its receivers, giving itself to them as goodness itself but also as the law" (DM 45/GD 41). Here it must be noted also that in the incarnation of goodness as law, the infinite being effaces itself. Thus when one reads that responsibility requires both that one respond as irreplaceable singularity and that one efface the origin of what one gives, one can read this effacement as encompassing both the infinite and the finite being. There is an effacing of the infinite being in its becoming finite/incarnate and an effacing of the finite/incarnated being. The reading of death—death as possibility turning into death as impossibility—that I suggested earlier should be read alongside responsibility in that moment of Patočka's genealogy called "Christianity" effects a transformation of the reading of revelation by drawing God out of objectivity, thereby keeping Patočka's reference to a supreme being distinct from all onto-theological meaning in the sense that Heidegger gave to it (DM 39/GD 33).

Derrida's reading of Patočka's genealogy of responsibility—which finds its fulfillment in the God of Christianity whose gift of goodness calls one to goodness—raises the question of the role of the demonic in Patočka's Christianity. Recall that according to Patočka's genealogy of responsibility—demonic or orgiastic mystery, Platonic mystery, Christian mystery—each conversion from one mystery to the next conserves something of what is interrupted. This logic of conservative rupture, Derrida suggests, resembles the economy of a sacrifice and sometimes reminds one of the economy of sublation (*relève*) or *Aufhebung*. Patočka employs the terms *incorporation* (*přivtělení*) and *repression* (*potlačení*) to describe this double conversion: Platonic mystery incorporates demonic or orgiastic mystery and Christian mystery represses Platonic mystery. This vocabulary indicates—if these words were meant to be given the meanings that they possess in psychoanalytic discourse—that in the conversion from one mystery to another the first is not destroyed, but kept inside unconsciously, after effecting a topical displacement and a hierarchical subordination (DM 18/GD 9). This language also suggests—again, if these words were meant to be given the meanings that they possess in psychoanalytic discourse—that conversion amounts to a process of mourning, to keeping within oneself that whose death must be endured (DM 18/GD 9). Derrida points out that in the conversion from demonic or orgiastic mystery to Platonic mystery, the mystery of the demonic is kept within oneself and endured (which, Derrida suggests, amounts to a process of mourning). "The secret of responsibility would consist of keeping secret, or 'incorporated,' the secret of the demonic and thus of preserving within itself a nucleus of irresponsibility or of absolute unconsciousness, something Patočka will later call 'orgiastic irresponsibility'" (DM 27/GD 20). Derrida is referring specifically to the conversion from demonic or orgiastic mystery to Platonic mystery, but there is no reason that the demonic does not recur in the Christian mystery.[8] "Orgiastic mystery recurs indefinitely, it is always at work: not only in Platonism, [. . .] but also in Christianity and even in the space of the *Aufklärung* and of secularization in general" (DM 28/GD 21). This preservation of the demonic in the Christian mystery contaminates the Christian mystery. The Christian mystery "will never become" (quoting Derrida, though with respect to the Platonic mystery and its incorporation of the demonic) "pure and authentic, or absolutely new" (DM 27/GD 20). Derrida's choice of words here echoes the aporetic character of Heidegger's existential analysis of death—death, the most proper possibility of Dasein, becomes the most improper possibility and the most ex-propriating, the most inauthenticating possibility (AM 337/AD 77). The aporias of death and responsibility characteristic of that moment of Patočka's genealogy of responsibility called "Christianity" attests, I would suggest, to the contamination of the God of infinite love by the demonic. It attests to the ruination of the conversion to Christianity (insofar as Christianity is understood as characterized *merely* by a God whose gift of goodness calls one to goodness) because the responsibility demanded of me holds me accountable and discounts me. Responsibility requires—using words of Blanchot that echo Heidegger's analysis of death as the possibility of the impossibility of Dasein—that I answer for the impossibility of being responsible, which makes me always already guilty or irresponsible. The God of Christianity calls one to goodness and badness, to responsibility and irresponsibility.

The contamination of the purity of the reference to a revelatory event by the nondogmatic doublet of dogma not only calls for a rereading of Christianity that opens a space for Patočka's "heretical and hyperbolic form" of Christianity, but also calls for a rereading of Judaism. Levinas offers a rereading of Judaism in his "confessional" work.

In the foreword to *Beyond the Verse*, Levinas responds to the question "Why beyond the verse?" Scriptures have a plain meaning that is also enigmatic. The implied meanings extricated from the meanings immediately offered have enigmas themselves, which sets in motion an incessant hermeneutics of inexhaustible verses. "A reading of Scripture, therefore, which is forever beginning again; a revelation which is forever continued" (AV 7/BV x). Levinas continues by drawing his reading of Descartes' *Meditations* into his reading of the revelatory event in Judaism. The great principle behind the often repeated Talmudic teaching "The Torah speaks the language of men" is, Levinas writes, the admission that the Word of God can be maintained in the language of created beings. How is it maintained? By "the marvelous contraction of the Infinite, the 'more' inhabiting the 'less,' the Infinite in the Finite, as in keeping with Descartes's 'idea of God'" (AV 7/BV x). Here one sees the enigmatic surplus of meaning that sets in motion an incessant hermeneutics of inexhaustible verses, a revelation which is forever continued. Unless, Levinas immediately adds (in a hesitation that he says does not impoverish the Cartesian idea but apparently complements it), the Word of God is maintained by the prophetic essence of language "capable of always signifying more than it says" (AV 7/BV x–xi), that is, capable of always signifying the "more" inhabiting the "less."

In "On the Jewish Reading of Scriptures," one of the texts of *Beyond the Verse*, Levinas writes that language, as inspired and calling for an exegetical reading that discovers the meaning that breaks through the immediate meaning, is the place of this overflowing of meaning, this interruption that awakens one to the other. It is the actual modality of the ethical code that disturbs the established order. With its referent as reading—"yet," Levinas adds, "no less wondrous for all that"—has one not discovered, he asks, the original figure of transcendence, a figure freed from the mythology of ulterior worlds? (AV 138/BV 111). Not only does Levinas's reference in the foreword to *Beyond the Verse* to the inspired essence of language, subsequent to his hesitation in the wake of his reference to Descartes' idea of the infinite, complement that reading of the maintenance of the Word of God in language, but it also precludes a too easy reading of that Cartesian idea, precludes, that is, a sedimented understanding of God as a transcendent being inhabiting an ulterior world and then inspiring texts of this world. Yet no sooner does he raise the issue of the original figure of transcendence freed from the mythology of ulterior worlds, then, in a move that echoes his reading of skepticism and the blinking light of revelation, he asks: Will a person not resist this reading of transcendence, a reading *already* impoverished from the perspective of a traditional reading, by reducing the transcendence of inspiration, exegesis, and the moral message, to merely one's interiority. As if to say, the cause of the transcendence is unequivocal: not the steady light of the transcendent as it is traditionally understood, but rather the steady light of one's own uninterrupted creative power. But Levinas then asks: "In order to dispute such modern-day resistance, would it not have been necessary to interpret as inspiration the reasons of reasoning reason in which philosophy, in its logic, recognizes the reign of Identity which nothing that is *other* could disrupt or guide?" (AV 140/BV 113). Using the vocabulary of his reading of skepticism, he writes that there is an incessant "alternation" between "the traumatic experience of the unknown and strange meaning" that disturbs one's sedimented and comforting ways of thinking and "the grammar which, already operating on another level, restores order, coherence and chronology." Here is "an alternation which, admittedly, testifies to the hesitation of our little faith, but from which also stems the transcendence that does not impose itself with denials through its actual coming and which, in inspired Scripture, awaits a hermeneutic—in other words, reveals itself only in dissimulation" (AV 142/BV 115). Here the steady beacon of revelation (whether it be unequivocal light of the theist *or* the atheist) that guides one out of the wilderness is reread as the blinking light of revelation. This rereading "testifies to the hesitation of our little faith."

This disturbing alternation is likewise maintained, I would suggest, in Levinas's rereading of the work of ritual. In another text from *Beyond the*

Verse, titled "Revelation in the Jewish Tradition," Levinas writes that Jewish revelation is based on the prescription of the Law. In the halakhic texts of the Talmud, strictly ethical laws are juxtaposed with the ritual prescriptions that govern all the acts of everyday life. And the highest action of the practice of prescriptions is, as Levinas notes, the actual study of the Law. "It is *as if*, in this study, man were in mystical contact with the divine will itself" (AV 170/BV 141, emphasis added). The "as if" here is significant, for it introduces an ambiguity into what otherwise may be taken as an unequivocal revelation of the transcendent. In ritual (and arguably the highest action of the practice of prescriptions—that is, the study of the Law—is likewise a ritual, perhaps the ritual of rituals) there is no unambiguous contact with that which is transcendent to nature. "In ritual a distance is taken up *within* nature *in respect of nature*, and perhaps therefore it is precisely the waiting for the Most-High which is a relation to Him—or, if one prefers, a deference, a deference to the beyond which creates here the very concept of a beyond or a towards-God [d'*à-Dieu*]" (AV 173/BV 143). The work of ritual is commonly seen as a moment in nature when nature is revealed in its truth, specifically, a moment in nature when the Most-High who transcends nature is revealed. This reading of ritual is not unlike the reading of the transformative power of death that effects a step beyond. But, for Levinas, the work of ritual is arguably read alongside the aporia of death—death as possibility turning into death as impossibility. Ritual is a movement in nature in which "a distance is taken up within nature in respect of nature." In the ritual of studying the Law, one discovers those moments in the work (the text of the Torah as well as the exegesis of that text) when one finds oneself at a distance from that work. "My condition—or my un-condition—is my relation to books. It is the very movement-towards-God [l'*à-Dieu*]" (AV 9/BV xii). Here one encounters a step/not beyond that opens up the space of dead time, the interval of the not yet. Here one encounters a creation of the very concept of the beyond, or more precisely, of a towards-God, an *à-Dieu*. Here one again encounters the blinking light of revelation in the production of a going *to God* that is, at the same time, a *good-bye*.

In "The Name of God according to a few Talmudic Texts" (among other texts), Levinas reads this ambiguous manifestation of God alongside the Law that obliges me to the other. The generic word *God* is, Levinas writes, absent from the Hebrew language. What is translated from the Hebrew terms of the Hebrew Scriptures as "God" in English are proper names according to the wishes of the Talmud. In fact, the first book of the Tractate in which Maimonides summarizes and systematizes the Talmud begins: "The foundation of the foundation and the pillar of wisdom consists in knowing that the Name exists and that it is the first being" (AV 147/BV 119). The divinity is designated by the generic term *Name* in relation to which the different proper names of God are individuals. To say "God" is in the Talmud to say "the Holy One, blessed be He," that is, the attribute *Holiness* (which in rabbinical thought evokes, above all, separation) preceded by a definite article. "The term thus names—and this is quite remarkable—a mode of being or a beyond of being rather than a quiddity" (AV 148/BV 119). Other words for God, such as *Shekhinah* (which means the dwelling of God in the world) likewise do not express essence, but relation. They indicate a way of being. And what precisely is its way of being? Its way of being is as ambiguity, as a blinking light of revelation. "The square letters," Levinas's reference to Hebrew, "are a precarious dwelling from which the revealed Name is already withdrawn" (AV 149/BV 121). The Name of the otherwise than being is, like the skeptical saying, a writing that "opens itself up to the search for its origin," the search for the condition of its enunciation, and in doing so, "becomes contemporaneous with the history which can be remembered and in which transcendence is cancelled out." But the refutation of the revealed Name, like the refutation of the skeptical saying, presupposes what the revealed Name (and the skeptical saying) calls into question, that is, the contemporaneousness of what would otherwise alternate. Like the skeptical saying, transcendence is canceled out, but it returns. This incessant alternation produces the trace of a past that was never present and, as such, can never be remembered. The withdrawal or canceling out of the transcendence of the revealed Name is "an epiphany bordering on atheism" (AV 149/BV 121). Given that this statement is situated within the context of the blinking light of revelation, Levinas could just as well have written: an epiphany bordering on theism. The interminable withdrawal of the Name is nothing other than its interminable approach. In either case, the Name does not, as Levinas has already pointed out, express essence.

This withdrawal (or approach) of the Name of God is the very commandment that obliges me toward all others. Levinas believes that this is the meaning of one of the Talmudic apologues grafted onto a verse in Genesis in connection to the question: must the names of God mentioned in the Hebrew Scriptures, such as *Adonai*, be treated as holy names? The answer is yes, particularly in those verses relating the story of Abraham. But in Genesis 18:3 the name *Adonai* is used to address one of the three angels who, in human form, appears to Abraham as an anonymous passer-by lost in the wilderness: "Adonai (Lord), if I have found favor in your sight, do not pass by your servant." To get out of the difficulty of apparently not treating *Adonai* as a holy name (because it is applied not to God but to an anonymous passer-by), an apologue is grafted onto this verse. According to the apologue, "Adonai, do not pass by your servant" is in fact addressed to God who is said to have appeared to Abraham at the same time as the passers-by. Abraham said to God: "Wait for me to receive the three travelers." This was said because the passers-by, overcome with heat and thirst, come before the Lord our God.

Levinas immediately adds: "The transcendence of God is his actual effacement, but this obliges us to men." Levinas then provocatively asks whether
this apologue, which he said the Talmud grafts onto Genesis 18:3, *is* a graft.
"Is not the meaning suggested already in the very fact of saying Lord, Adonai,
to an anonymous passer-by lost in the wilderness? Is not the apologue merely
paying extreme attention to the letter of the text?" (AV 153–4/BV 124–25). Is
not the meaning of the apologue (that is, the transcendence of the Name of
God is God's effacement, which is the commandment that obliges me to the
other), already suggested in saying "Adonai" to an anonymous passer-by lost
in the wilderness? Levinas seems to suggest that there is a slippage between
God and the other person.

This rereading of the revelatory event in Judaism is a moment, I would
suggest, in the double origin of the logical and philosophical deduction of religious themes such as responsibility and the religious event of revelation. This
double origin, considered in Derrida's *The Gift of Death* and *Aporias*, raises
the question of the relationship between Levinas's "confessional" work
(which testifies to the faith experience of a revelatory event) and his "philosophical" work. Levinas insists that he always makes a "clear distinction"
between the two (DEL 18). But along with his admission that "they may ultimately have a common source of inspiration" (DEL 18), could one say (using
the words of Derrida) that "one implies the other" (DM 53/GD 50)? That is,
is there an "irreducibly double inclusion" operative here (AM 338/AD 80)?

Levinas himself approaches this possibility, though only in the form of
a denial, that this double origin is operative in his work. Everything comes to
pass, Derrida writes with respect to his reading of Patočka, as though the logical and philosophical deduction of responsibility were ultimately capable of
producing Christianity. Yet it can also be said, with equal validity, that Christianity has made possible access to authentic responsibility. In "Revelation in
the Jewish Tradition," Levinas approaches a similar structure of thinking.
Toward the end of the text he comes to the "main problem." It is not a problem of the revealed contents confessed by revealed religions requiring authen-
tication; that is, it is not a problem of the revealed contents requiring a rational justification that would be closed in upon itself, undisturbed by anything
outside its rational self-sufficiency of reason. It is a problem about the possibility of a rupture of the closed order of totality or of its correlative, reason,
which would not alienate the self-sufficiency of reason. Levinas wonders
"whether there are not aspects in Judaism which indicate the 'rationality' of a
reason less turned in upon itself than the reason of philosophical tradition"
(AV 176/BV 146). He then offers a few examples from the Judaic tradition.
After beginning with the revealed (though dissimulated) content of Judaism,
he explains that not to begin with the inheritance of Greek philosophy does
not mean that he is rejecting it, or that he will not have recourse to it later, or

that he is giving way to mysticism. He in fact implicitly refers to his recourse to this tradition (albeit as one moment of an irreducibly ambiguous reading) when, in the wake of his consideration of Judaism, he mentions the infinite responsibility to the other in his philosophical texts. Given the order of presentation, he seems to suggest that the revealed content of Judaism makes possible access to authentic responsibility. He then (nearly) reverses the order of presentation by suggesting that it is as though the philosophical deduction of responsibility were capable of producing the revealed content of Judaism. "Admittedly," Levinas writes, "it is not a matter of deducing from this responsibility the *actual* content of the Bible: Moses and the prophets" (AV 177/BV 147, emphasis added). In denying that one can deduce the actual figures of Moses and the prophets from the responsibility considered in his philosophical texts, perhaps Levinas is leaving open the possibility that one can deduce from this responsibility Judaism's exegesis of the *revealed message* of Moses and the prophets. Even if this suggestion is a bit labored, it remains that the trajectory of the narrative of "Revelation in the Jewish Tradition" at least approaches a consideration of the double origin of the logical and philosophical deduction of responsibility and responsibility as a revealed content of Judaism.

Levinas's rereading of the revelatory event in Judaism is coupled with a rereading of the particularity of the Jewish people given by election. This election is read alongside the aporias of death and responsibility. That is, the singularity of election (a moment in the aporia of responsibility coupled with the singularity given by death as possibility) is coupled with an absolute exposure to the other, a being nothing but "for the other" (which is a moment in the aporia of responsibility coupled with the ex-propriation given by death as impossibility). In a text from *Difficult Freedom* titled "A Religion for Adults," Levinas writes: "This election is made up not of privileges but of responsibilities. It is a nobility based not on royalties or a birthright conferred by a divine caprice, but on the position of each human I." The position of the singular I is an asymmetrical relation with the other in which "I see myself *obligated* with respect to the Other; consequently I am infinitely more demanding of myself than of others." Then, quoting a talmudic text that is echoed in his reading of responsibility alongside death in *Totality and Infinity*, Levinas writes: "The more just I am, the more harshly I am judged" (DL 39/DF 22; see TeI 222/TaI 244). Election, for Levinas, means "a surplus of duties" (AV 152/BV 123). It means that the singular I is, paradoxically, nothing but "for the other," which overflows the capabilities of the necessary (yet necessarily interrupted) singular I. It is this reading of election coupled with exposure to the other that opens up an understanding of what Levinas calls "Jewish universalism" (DL 38/DF 21). In "Judaism and Revolution," from *From the Sacred to the Holy*, Levinas writes that the heirs of Abraham are "men to whom their ancestor bequeathed a difficult tradition of duties toward the other man, which one is never done with, an order in which one is never free." Defined in this way, the heirs of Abraham "are of all nations: any man truly man is no doubt of the line of Abraham" (SS 19/NTR 99). Everyone, insofar as they have received the Law that is simultaneously election and exposure to the other, is an heir of Abraham. Here the recoil of the "nondogmatic doublet of dogma" back upon the "traditional" reading of the revelatory event effects an opening of the singular dogma of Judaism to a certain universality.

Levinas's rereading of the revelatory event of Judaism raises the question of its proximity to Patočka's rereading of the revelatory event of Christianity. There are, to be sure, significant differences between the revelatory events of Judaism and those of Christianity (Levinas has on occasion mentioned these differences). But there is also a moment of convergence. Both Levinas's rereading and Patočka's rereading are attentive to the aporia of responsibility (which must be read alongside the aporia of death), that moment when the singular I turns into the absolute effacement of oneself in being nothing but obliged to the other, that moment when God's effacement is the Law that obliges the singular I to the other. At that moment, if only for a moment, one can think together the work of Levinas and Patočka. This is not done out of ignorance of the essential differences between the revelatory events that these two thinkers articulate. It is done with an attentiveness to those decisive moments in their work on the *work of the revelatory event* when work is discovered to be at a certain distance from that work.

In *The Gift of Death* Derrida next extends his consideration of the aporias of death and responsibility to a reading of Genesis 22. The *Akedah* "belongs to what one might just dare to call the common treasure, the terrifying secret of the *mysterium tremendum* that is a property of all three so-called religions of the Book [that is, Judaism, Christianity, and Islam], the religions of the races of Abraham" (DM 65/GD 64).

This reading of Genesis 22 is, I would suggest, a supplement to Levinas's reading of irresponsibility as a modality of responsibility. Up to this point the couple responsibility/irresponsibility has been considered only with respect to the asymmetrical relationship of the self and the other. It has not played a role in the relationship of the self with the other other. Derrida's reading of Genesis 22 considers the role of the couple responsibility/irresponsibility in the relationship of the self with the other other.

What makes one tremble in the *mysterium tremendum* of Patočka's Christian responsibility is the gift of infinite love, the dissymmetry between the divine regard that sees me, and myself, who does not see the hidden, silent, and secret God, all of which is logically deduced from the disproportion between the experience of responsibility as irreplaceability (which is given in death read as possibility) and the experience of responsibility that is the forgetting or effacement of oneself (which is given, I have suggested, in death read as impossibility) (DM 58/GD 55–56).

Derrida uses this consideration of trembling to segue to Kierkegaard's *Fear and Trembling*. The *mysterium tremendum*, like the title of Kierkegaard's work, includes "at least an implicit and indirect reference" (DM 58/GD 56) to a passage in Philippians: "Therefore, my beloved, as you have always obeyed, so now, not only as in my presence but much more in my absence, work out your own salvation with fear and trembling" (Philippians 2:12, Revised Standard Version). The disciples are asked to work out their own salvation in the absence of the master. Here Derrida recalls his earlier consideration of the shift noted by him in Heidegger's *Being and Time* from *abnehmen* to *aufnehmen* in the sense of *auf sich nehmen*. The death that cannot be taken away (*abnehmen*) must be taken upon oneself (*auf sich nehmen*). I must appropriate death, I must assume this possibility of impossibility, if I am to have access to what is irreplaceably mine (this appropriation of death, it is important to recall, is characteristic of the first moment in the genealogy of death—death as possibility). To this first explanation of fear and trembling Derrida adds that if Paul says "adieu" as he asks the community to obey, in fact ordering them to obey, "it is because God is himself absent, hidden and silent, separate, secret, at the moment he has to be obeyed" (DM 59/GD 57). God does not give reasons; otherwise God would not be God as wholly other. Paul continues: "[F]or God is at work in you, both to will and to work for his good pleasure" (Philippians 2:13, Revised Standard Version). In a footnote to this passage Derrida notes that "his good pleasure" does not refer to God's pleasure but to God's sovereign will "that is not required to consult, just as the king acts as he intends without revealing his secret reasons, without having to account for his actions or explain them" (DM 107n5/GD 57n3).

In *Fear and Trembling* Kierkegaard considers a double secret in God's commanding Abraham to sacrifice his son Isaac (Genesis 22): the secret between God and Abraham and the secret between Abraham and his family. When Isaac asks where the sacrificial lamb is to be found, Abraham responds while keeping the secret: "God will provide himself the lamb for a burnt offering, my son" (Genesis 22:8, Revised Standard Version). This double secret also involves the double necessity of keeping the secret—Abraham must keep the secret because it is his duty, and he must keep the secret because, as Derrida notes, he can do nothing but keep it (DM 60/GD 59) insofar as he does not know it.

Derrida writes, within the context of his consideration of Genesis 22, that responsibility demands absolute singularity and substitution (DM 62/GD 61). But these two demands are contradictory, for the general answering-for-oneself in the medium of language and the concept before the generality of others, the translation of absolute singularity into universal principles, suspends my absolute responsibility to God. By translating the decision from the "solitary, secret, and silent" into the general by answering for myself in the public arena, that is, by suspending my absolute irreplaceable singularity, I renounce my freedom and absolute responsibility. This translation into what Kierkegaard calls the "ethical" is always a temptation (DM 62/GD 61). In the "instant of decision" one is absolutely singular. One is a singular person that has an absolute responsibility to a singular other. Falling back on precedents or universal principles serves only to *generalize* the situation which makes one irresponsible (but it is important to keep in mind that not generalizing the situation, that is, not responding to the other other also makes one irresponsible). As soon as one succumbs to the temptation of the ethical, one loses that irreplaceable singularity given by death (one also loses, it is important to note, the ex-propriation, the substitution likewise given by death and likewise required by absolute responsibility). It is as if absolute responsibility must be irresponsible to be absolutely responsible. It must transgress the ethical order, which for Kierkegaard stands for Hegelian *Sittlichkeit* (but also arguably includes Kantian *Moralität*). It must be irresponsible insofar as it must not answer for itself (that is, before the law of some universal tribunal); it must resist translation into the general; it must remain un*concept*ualizable (DM 62/GD 61); it must remain un*present*able. Abraham presents himself before God, the one to whom he says, "Here I am," at the same time as he refuses to present himself before the community (DM 63/GD 62).

The necessity yet impossibility of thinking the two moments of the paradox together "remains irreducible to presence or to presentation, it demands a temporality of the instant without ever constituting a present" (DM 66/GD 65). It demands the "atemporal temporality" (DM 66/GD 65) of the instant, a duration that cannot be stabilized; it cannot be grasped or comprehended. With every genuine decision, there is, if only for an instant, a suspension of comprehension. There is, if only for an instant, a suspension of the work of negation and the work itself. The work of absolute responsibility is inevitably irresponsible. To put one's faith in God to work, that is, to assume one's absolute responsibility, one must be guilty or irresponsible, one must transgress ethical duty. But in transgressing it one belongs to it and at the same time recognizes it. "Abraham must assume absolute responsibility for sacrificing his son by sacrificing ethics, but in order for there to be a sacrifice, the ethical must retain all its value" (DM 66/GD 66). Abraham's love for his son Isaac must remain intact at the same time as the ethical expression for what he does is: he hates Isaac (FB 122/FT 74). Here one sees the ruination of the step that is the work of absolute responsibility *in the performance of the step itself.* Here one sees the unworking of the work of absolute responsibility. Every genuine decision demands the sacrifice (and, at the same time, the recognition) of the ethical order, if only for an instant. The necessary yet impossible paradox "must be endured *in the instant itself*' (DM 66/GD 66). The aporia must be endured. But what does this mean? One cannot underestimate the profound unworking at the heart of this work of enduring the aporia. In *Aporias*, following his rereading of Heidegger's existential analysis of death considered earlier, Derrida writes: "[I]f one must endure the aporia, if such is the law of all decisions, of all responsibilities, of all duties without duty, and of all the border problems that ever can arise, *the aporia can never simply be endured as such*. The ultimate aporia is the impossibility of the aporia *as such*" (AM 337/AD 78). Quoting Kierkegaard, Derrida writes: "[T]he instant of decision is madness" (DM 66/GD 65). It is important to note that madness does not arise because one has a choice between two different but equally plausible choices. It is rather the case that choosing one is choosing the other, being responsible is transgressing responsibility, being responsible is being irresponsible, if only for an instant. If a decision did not involve a sacrifice of ethics, that is, if a decision were merely between two extant choices, no "call to action" or "call of conscience" would be unconditional. The decision would be generalized. It would be comfortably situated within past or present contexts of origination or within future horizons of expectation. For example, "I made that decision because, given the circumstances, it was the best decision," or "I made that decision because it will further my (future) salvation." With this stabilization of the aporia, an ethics of good conscience reinstalls itself. One is obliged to behave not only in a responsible manner, but also in an irresponsible manner, and one is obliged to do that *in the name of* absolute duty (DM 67/GD 67). And this name which must always be singular is, as Derrida points out, the name of God as absolutely other to which I am bound by an absolute obligation (DM 67/GD 67). "God is the name of the absolute other as other and as unique (the God of Abraham defined as the one and unique)" (DM 68/GD 68).

The aporia of responsibility is complicated by the formula *tout autre est tout autre*, every other (one) is every (bit) other, which disturbs Kierkegaard's discourse on the absolute uniqueness of Jahweh (DM 77/GD 79) while pushing it to its logical conclusion, because it implies that the wholly other God is everywhere one finds the wholly other. "And since each of us, everyone else, each other is infinitely other in its absolute singularity, inaccessible, solitary, transcendent, nonmanifest, originarily nonpresent to my *ego* [. . .], then what can be said about Abraham's relation to God can be said about my relation without relation [*rapport sans rapport*] to *every other* (one) *as every* (bit) *other* [*tout autre comme tout autre*], in particular my relation to my neighbor or my loved ones who are as inaccessible to me, as secret and transcendent as Jahweh" (DM 76–77/GD 78).[9] God—serving as the index not only of the *wholly other* (*tout autre*) but also of *every* (other) *other* (*tout autre*)—is other than himself; God is his "own" other (and given that this perhaps calls into question

God's gender and personhood, perhaps it would be more appropriate to write that God is other than him/her/itself, God is his/her/its own other). But is not God, as Levinas maintains in "God and Philosophy," "not simply the 'first other,' the 'other par excellence,' or the 'absolutely other,' but other than the other, other otherwise, other with an alterity prior to the alterity of the other, prior to the ethical bond with another and different from every neighbor?" (DP 115/GP 165–66). Perhaps. But is it not this uncertainty that constitutes the other as wholly other? Otherwise would not the wholly other be an apodictic notion, something clear and distinct, rather than something to be believed?

The border between the religious and the ethical—a border that both Kierkegaard and Levinas want to maintain—becomes, therefore, questionable. If every other (one) is every (bit) other (*tout autre est tout autre*), then Kierkegaard can no longer distinguish between a generality of ethics (that would need to be sacrificed) and the faith that turns toward God alone (and away from human duty), since what Kierkegaard calls "ethics" is also (as Levinas reminds him) the order of and respect for absolute singularity (that is, ethics is not only the order of generality). Therefore, Kierkegaard cannot distinguish between the ethical order and the religious order. But in taking into account the absolute alterity in relations between one human being and another, Levinas likewise can no longer distinguish between the alterity of God and the "same" alterity of every human being (which he wants to do). He likewise can no longer determine the limit between the ethical order and the religious order. "His ethics is already a religious one" (DM 81/GD 84). Levinas, therefore, cannot say something completely different from Kierkegaard, and vice versa.

The trembling of the formula *tout autre est tout autre* circles back upon the earlier reading of Patočka's Christianity. Recall that in the conversion from Platonism to Christianity the Good is no longer a transcendental objective, but the relation to the other. It is "an experience of personal goodness and a movement of intention" (DM 54/GD 50). This goodness is a goodness that forgets itself, and this movement is a movement of the gift that renounces itself, that is, a movement of infinite love. "Only infinite love," Derrida writes, "can renounce itself and, in order to *become finite*, become incarnated in order to love the other, to love the other as a finite other" (DM 54/GD 51). Could one, perhaps, read the phrase *tout autre est tout autre* as an articulation of the infinite *becoming* finite, because as radically other, God is other than him/her/itself?

The trembling of the formula *tout autre est tout autre* also calls for a rereading of the relationship between Levinas's reading of the alterity of the infinite in Descartes' *Meditations* and Levinas's reading of the alterity of the other person. This relationship is ambiguous. Is Levinas' reading of Descartes' *Meditations* merely a formal reading of the idea of infinity that then needs to be deformalized or concretized in the face (TeI 21/TaI 50)? Is the subject's relationship with the infinite as it is articulated in Descartes' *Meditations* maintained at a distance from the subject's relationship with the other person? With the formula *tout autre est tout autre*, the relationship with God serves as an index of not only the *wholly other* (*tout autre*) but also of *every* (other) *other* (*tout autre*). This formula helps to articulate better the relationship between Levinas's reading of the alterity of the infinite in Descartes' *Meditations* and Levinas's reading of the alterity of the other person, but it comes at the expense, as was mentioned earlier, of the distinction Levinas attempts to maintain between the alterity of God and the alterity of every human being (DM 81/GD 84).

The ambiguity of the word *à-Dieu* serves to gather together many of the ideas considered up to this moment. Recall that only the aporia of death—that moment when death as possibility turns into death as impossibility—is adequate to the aporia of responsibility, insofar as death as possibility gives irreplaceable singularity and death as impossibility gives the ex-propriation, the anonymity, that is a forgetting or effacement of oneself. The aporia of responsibility calls for being read alongside the aporia of death. The more I am responsible, the more I am irresponsible, guilty, because responsibility holds me accountable and discounts me. This irresponsibility at the heart of responsibility is compounded in the reading of Genesis 22. It is as though in the singular relationship with the singular other (God), which already involves irresponsibility, one is inevitably implicated in another form of irresponsibility—the sacrifice of the other other, the others other than God. Therefore, in absolute responsibility a going *to God* and a *good-bye* coincide: *à-Dieu*. The *à-Dieu* serves to gather together several movements. This "good-bye" of/to God has several different (are they different?) trajectories: (1) good-bye of/to God as palpably present insofar as God is absent, hidden and silent, separate, secret, at the moment that God has to be obeyed (DM 59/GD 57), (2) good-bye of/to God as transcendent insofar as God becomes its own other, becomes finite, becomes incarnated as command (DM 45, 54/GD 41, 51), with the self thereby becoming its own other, and (3) good-bye of/to God as transcendent guarantee of the Good, of responsibility, insofar as God becomes its own other, that is, the demonic, the *il y a*. The *à-Dieu* marks the aporia that responsibility *has* to be transgressed *in the name of* an absolute obligation to God, which merely serves as an index of not only the *wholly other* (*tout autre*) but also of *every* (other) *other* (*tout autre*). The *à-Dieu* marks the moment when a linear movement oriented in the direction of a goal, a production, a work, finds itself at a distance from itself, is interrupted.

The *à-Dieu* also marks the opening of the space of community. This opening will be traced beginning with Derrida's rereading of the existential analysis of death in *Being and Time*, which opens up the space of community within the context of raising the question of the proximity of the work of Heidegger and Levinas. Levinas objects to what he, Levinas, perceives as the privileging of Dasein's proper death in Heidegger's existential analytic. Levinas reminds us, Derrida points out, that the other's death, rather than my own, is the "first death" (MT 38; AM 323/AD 39). Levinas writes: "I am responsible for the death of the other to the extent of including myself in that death. That can be shown in a more acceptable proposition: 'I am responsible for the other inasmuch as the other is mortal.' It is the other's death that is the foremost death" (MT 38). The question of whether my death or the death of the other is first is rendered irresolvably ambiguous by Derrida's rereading of Heidegger's analysis of death as possibility of the impossibility of Dasein. The relation to the disappearing as such of the "as such"—the "as such" that Heidegger makes the distinctive mark and the specific ability of Dasein (that is, the authentic, resolute, determinate, and decided assumption of death)—is also the characteristic common, according to Derrida, *both* to the inauthentic *and* to the authentic forms of the existence of Dasein, common to all experiences of death (perishing, demising, and properly dying) (AM 336/AD 75). As such, Dasein never has a relation to dying as such, but only to perishing, to demising, and, thereby, to the death of the other (AM 336/AD 76). "The death of the other," Derrida writes, obviously referring to the work of Levinas, "thus becomes again 'first,' always first" (AM 336/AD 76). The "first" here is presumably placed in quotation marks to indicate that the priority of the death of the other (over the death of oneself) is, though opened up by Derrida's reading, not definitively determined. Therefore, rather than writing that Dasein never has a relation to dying as such, but only to perishing, to demising, and, thereby, to the death of the other, would it perhaps be more precise to write that in dying as such, Dasein is opened to perishing, to demising, and, thereby, to the death of the other? That is, it seems as though rather than merely reversing the polarity, one is left with an irreducible ambiguity. What remains is an irreducible paradox.

In dying as such (which, according to one reading, constitutes the self of the *Jemeinigkeit*; DM 49/GD 45), Dasein is opened to the death of the other, to mourning (which, according to another reading, constitutes the self of the *Jemeinigkeit*; AM 336/AD 76). In my death, that is, in dying as such, I am opened to the death of the other. My being-for-death is always already mediated (or rather, as Derrida suggests, "immediately mediatizable") in the "non-experienceable" structure of impossible mourning (P 321–22). This is what Derrida calls "ex-appropriation," that is, appropriation caught in a double bind (P 321). Mourning is an unfaithful fidelity (compare with: death is an impossible possibility, and responsibility is an irresponsible responsibility) in that, according to *Memoires for Paul de Man*, it is where "*success fails*" and "*failure succeeds*" (MpP 54/MfP 35). What does this mean? Since Freud, the normal work of mourning is described as an interiorization of the other, an attempt to keep the other in me, in memory. Faithful interiorization is unfaithful in that it effaces the radical otherness of the other. Unfaithful interiorization is faithful in that it respects the radical otherness of the other. In mourning one is "obliged to harbor something that is greater and other" than oneself (MpP 54/MfP 34). Here one sees ex-appropriation that is not unlike Levinas's description of the idea of infinity in his reading of Descartes' *Meditations*, where according to the chronological order the other is in me and according to the "logical" order the other is outside me. "If *Jemeinigkeit*, that of *Dasein* or that of the ego (in the common sense, the psychoanalytic sense, or Levinas's sense) is constituted in its ipseity in terms of an originary mourning, then this self-relation welcomes or supposes the other within its being-itself as different from itself. And reciprocally: the relation to the other (in itself outside myself, outside myself in myself) will never be distinguishable from a bereaved apprehension" (AM 331/AD 61).

If the relation to the other is indistinguishable from a bereaved apprehension, then according to the "logic" of the formula *tout autre est tout autre*, does this include God? That is, is the relation to God indistinguishable from a bereaved apprehension? Is there a mourning of the death of God that is articulated by *à-Dieu*?

It is important to note that the opening of the space of community in the death of the other—an opening marked by an *à-Dieu*—does not produce anything. Just as what is produced in Levinas's reading of Descartes' *Meditations* is not something that unambiguously appears, but rather an irreducible ambiguity, a trace of what calls into question what appears, so death (a concretization of Levinas's reading of Descartes' *Meditations*) is the unworking of any work produced. "Community necessarily takes place in what Blanchot has called 'unworking,' referring to that which, before or beyond the work, withdraws from the work, and which, no longer having to do either with production or with completion, encounters interruption, fragmentation, suspension" (CD 78–79/IC 31). One must be careful, therefore, not to hypostatize community. Opened by the death of the other, the community is characterized by an incompletion, a not yet, that incessantly unworks the teleology that would gather a community together without absolving the community of making such ties. The unworking of the community "puts an end to the hopes of the groups" (CI 38/UC 20).

Abraham's *à-Dieu* is without hope. *In* the necessary yet impossible enduring of the aporia of responsibility, Abraham renounced hope (DM 72/GD 72). Here one sees an unworking in the heart of the work of responsibility. Here one sees a community of faith founded on a renunciation of hope. *In* the unworking of the work of responsibility, one is called (borrowing the words of T. S. Eliot) to "wait without hope / For hope would be hope for the wrong thing" (*Four Quartets*). However, this unworking in the heart of the work of responsibility does not absolve one of doing the work of responsibility. What does this mean practically? Perhaps not much. Perhaps nothing more (but is it that obvious or that easy?) than the vocation of incessant questioning that is philosophy itself.

Notes

1. THE INFINITE AND THE EVIL GENIUS: READING DESCARTES' *MEDITATIONS ON FIRST PHILOSOPHY*

1. This is *not* Levinas's phrase. It is borrowed from Derrida who uses it in a different context in "Ellipsis" (EeD 435/WaD 299).

2. Robert Bernasconi, "The Silent Anarchic World of the Evil Genius," in *The Collegium Phaenomenologicum: The First Ten Years*, 257–72, ed. John C. Sallis, Giuseppina Moneta, and Jacques Taminiaux (Dordrecht: Martinus Nijhoff, 1988), 265.

3. Levinas also refers to dead time in "The Infinity of Time" of *Totality and Infinity*:

> Being is no longer produced [*se produit*] at one blow, irremissibly present. Reality is what it is, but will be once again, another time freely resumed and pardoned. Infinite being is produced [*se produit*] as times, that is, in several times across the dead time [*le temps mort*] that separates the father from the son. It is not the finitude of being that constitutes the essence of time, as Heidegger thinks, but its infinity. The death sentence [*L'arrêt de la mort*] does not approach as an end of being, but as an unknown, which as such suspends power. The constitution of the interval that liberates being from the limitation of fate calls for death. The nothingness of the interval—a dead time [*un temps mort*]—is the production [*production*] of infinity. (TeI 260/TaI 284)

Levinas also refers to dead time in *Otherwise than Being or Beyond Essence*: "The expression 'in one's skin' is not a metaphor for the in-itself; it refers to a recurrence in the dead time [*le temps mort*] or the *meanwhile* which separates inspiration and expiration, the diastole and systole of the heart beating dully against the walls of one's skin" (AE 138/OB 109). Another notable reference to dead time occurs in Maurice Blanchot's *The Space of Literature*:

> In the region we are trying to approach, here has collapsed into nowhere, but nowhere is nonetheless here, and this empty, dead time [*le temps mort*] is a real time in which death is present—in which death happens but doesn't stop happening, as if, by happening, it rendered sterile the time in which it could happen. The dead present is the impossibility of making any presence real—an impossibility which is present, which is there as the present's double, the shadow of the present which the present bears and hides in itself. When I am alone, I am not alone, but, in this present, I am already returning to myself in the form of Someone. Someone is there, where I am alone. The fact of being alone is my belonging to this dead time [*ce temps mort*] which is not my time, or yours, or the time we share in common, but Someone's time. Someone is what is still present when there is no one. Where I am alone, I am not there; no one is there, but the impersonal is: the outside, as that which prevents, precedes, and dissolves the possibility of any personal relation. Someone is the faceless third person, the They of which everybody and anybody is part, but who is part of it? Never anyone in particular, never you and I. Nobody is part of the They. "They" belongs to a region which cannot be brought to light, not because it hides some secret alien to any revelation or even because it is radically obscure, but because it transforms everything which has access to it, even light, into anonymous, impersonal being, the Nontrue, the Nonreal yet always there. The They is, in this respect, what appears up very close when someone dies. (EL 23–24/SL 31)

Dead time is also referred to in Jacques Derrida's *Of Grammatology*: "Arche-writing as spacing cannot occur *as such* within the phenomenological experience of a *presence*. It marks *the dead time* [*le temps mort*] within the presence of the living present, within the general form of all presence. The dead time [*Le temps mort*] is at work" (DG 99/OG 68).

4. The English translators of "God and Philosophy" use the Haldane and Ross translation of Descartes' philosophical works. The Cottingham, Stoothoff, and Murdoch translation of this sentence reads: "[M]y perception of the infinite, that is God, is in some way prior to my perception of the finite, that is myself" (MPP 45/MFP 31).

5. Recall that Descartes explicitly states that the infinite is not the result of the formal structure of a negative judgment. "And I must not think that, just as my conceptions of rest and darkness are arrived at by negating movement and light, so my perception of the infinite is arrived at not by means of a true idea but merely by negating the finite" (MPP 45/MFP 31). Levinas recognizes this when he writes: "[I]t is as though the negation of the finite included in In-finity did not signify any sort of negation resulting from the formal structure of negative judgment" (DP 105–6/GP 160). In a footnote Levinas adds: "The latent birth of negation occurs not in subjectivity, but in the idea of the Infinite. Or, if one prefers, it is in subjectivity qua idea of the Infinite.

It is in this sense that the idea of the Infinite, as Descartes affirms, is a 'genuine idea' and not merely what I conceive 'by the negation of what is finite'" (DP 106n5/GP 160n6). The English translators of "God and Philosophy" use the Haldane and Ross translation of Descartes' philosophical works rather than the Cottingham, Stoothoff, and Murdoch translation quoted earlier.

3. THE BODY AND THE (NON)SENSE IN SENSIBILITY

1. Levinas writes: "The Husserlian thesis of the primacy of the objectifying act—in which was seen Husserl's excessive attachment to theoretical consciousness, and which has served as a pretext to accuse Husserl of intellectualism (as though that were an accusation!)—leads to transcendental philosophy" (TeI 95/TaI 123). Levinas is here alluding to himself as an interpreter of Husserl. In *The Theory of Intuition in Husserl's Phenomenology*, Levinas writes:

> Let us indicate at once [. . .] that although intuition appears as a very broad notion which makes no presuppositions about the mode of existence of its object, one should not forget that, for Husserl, intuition is a theoretical act, and that inasmuch as other acts can reach being they must, according to the *Logische Untersuchungen*, be based on a representation. [. . .] If *Ideen* modifies, with respect to the *Logische Untersuchungen*, the thesis according to which representation is the basis of all acts, it does not modify it enough to forbid us to say that each position of being (thesis) includes a representative thesis. We must, therefore, observe first that, for Husserl, being is correlative to theoretical intuitive life, to the evidence of an *objectifying act*. This is why the Husserlian concept of intuition is tainted with intellectualism and is possibly too narrow. (TdI 141/ToI 94)

2. Immediately following this passage, Levinas writes: "Separation has to be able to account for this constitutive conditioning accomplished [*accompli*] by representation—though representation be produced *after the event* [*se produire après coup*]" (TeI 143/TaI 169).

First, it seems as though Levinas's use of the term *production* here merely indicates that representation is conditioned, that it is posterior to life.

Second, separation has to be able to account for or accommodate representation's constituting, which moves on straight ahead, and its calling itself into question when it recognizes that what it constitutes is the condition of its constituting. That is, any account of the event of separation has to be able to account for or accommodate the distinction Levinas makes between knowledge or theory understood as comprehension and the critical essence of knowing, which, in its tracing back to a condition of comprehension, calls comprehension into question.

> The theoretical, being after the event [*après coup*], being essentially memory, is to be sure not creative; but its critical essence—its retrogressive movement—is no wise a possibility of enjoyment and labor. [It is not entirely clear what Levinas means when he writes that the critical essence of the theoretical is not to be

confounded with any possibility of enjoyment and labor. Perhaps he is reading enjoyment as freedom (TeI 59/TaI 87), which is *then* called into question by the critical essence of knowing.] It evinces a new energy, oriented upstream, counter-current, which the impassiveness of contemplation expresses only superficially. (TeI 143–44/TaI 169)

These two inversely oriented aspects of thought are articulated by the two movements of Levinas's reading of Descartes' *Meditations*. The two distinct movements of the *Meditations* characterize the very meaning of separation (TeI 19/TaI 48). The event of separation is, therefore, able to account for or accommodate the ambiguity of representation as condition and conditioned in that it is produced by representation's accomplishment of this inversion of order. The event of separation both accounts for and is accounted for by representation's accomplishment of this inversion of order. There is a reciprocity here that calls into question Levinas's use of the language of causality. It raises the question: what accounts for what? *This* reciprocity is reflected in the next paragraph of the text where Levinas writes that the ambiguity of representation as condition and conditioned—which is articulated by the inversely oriented movements of comprehension and critique—both results from and produces separation.

   3. This is attested to not only in "Representation and Constitution" and "Enjoyment and Nourishment," but also in the opening sentence of the next paragraph in the text: "The possibility of a representation that is constitutive but already rests on the enjoyment of a real completely constituted indicates the radical character of the uprootedness of him who is recollected in a home, where the I, while steeped in the elements, takes up its position before a Nature" (TeI 144/TaI 169).

   4. *This* articulation of separation, which is synonymous with the production of separation, is different from an articulation of separation that takes place after production, that is, after the progression through the two movements (for example, the description of the *cogito* as not yet, the posteriority of the anterior, etc., see especially TeI 25/TaI 54).

   5. It is interesting to note that despite the fact that Levinas establishes the proximity of Husserlian representation and the Cartesian clear and distinct idea (TeI 96–97/TaI 123–24), Levinas recognizes the superiority of Cartesian philosophy over Husserlian phenomenology which puts no limits on noematization. "The body indigent and naked is [the] very changing of sense. This is the profound insight Descartes had when he refused to sense data the status of clear and distinct ideas, ascribed them to the body, and relegated them to the useful. This is his superiority over Husserlian phenomenology which puts no limit on noematization" (TeI 102–3/TaI 129–30).

   6. This distinction parallels, I would suggest, the two movements integral to the production of separation or dwelling—the independence of the I of representation and the dependence upon the elemental. Earlier in *Totality and Infinity* Levinas describes dwelling in terms of "standing": "Dwelling is the very mode of *maintaining oneself* [*se tenir*], not as the famous serpent grasping itself by biting onto its tail, but as the body that, on the earth exterior to it, holds *itself* up [*se tient*] and can. The 'at home' [*Le*

«*chez soi*»] is not a container but a site where *I can*, where, dependent on a reality that is other [*autre*], I am, despite this dependence or thanks to it, free" (TeI 7/TaI 37). Standing, taken in abstraction or "detached from the conditions of its latent birth" (TeI 99/TaI 126), articulates representational thinking. But standing is always already a standing there, a standing on the earth, a being steeped in the elemental. Standing *there*, that is, standing *not* taken in abstraction, articulates "the radical character of the uprootedness of him who is recollected in a home" (TeI 144/TaI 169), for it articulates both the independence of the I of representation and the dependence upon the elemental, neither merely one nor the other. As an articulation of the not yet of the I of representation and the not yet of the elemental, it is otherwise than merely thinking. Hence, Levinas writes:

> Standing there [*S'y tenir*] is precisely different from "thinking." The bit of earth that supports me is not only my object; it supports my experience of objects. Well-trampled places do not resist me but support me. The relation with my site in this "stance" [«*tenue*»] precedes thought and labor. The body, position, the fact of standing [*se tenir*]—patterns of the primary relation with myself, of my coincidence with myself—nowise resemble idealist representation. (TeI 111/TaI 138)

Levinas is perhaps a bit too unequivocal when in this passage he writes that the body, the fact of standing—both of which are characterized by the same irreducible equivocality—nowise resemble idealist representation, for standing (not taken in abstraction) is, as I suggested above, an articulation of both the independence of the I of representation and the dependence upon the elemental, neither merely one nor the other. Therefore, rather than completely discounting idealist representation, it must be taken as one moment of the equivocation characteristic of the body, one moment of the fact of standing. Levinas himself seems to indicate this in the passage just quoted when he writes: "The bit of earth that supports me is *not only* my object; it supports my experience of objects" (TeI 111/TaI 138, emphasis added). By conceding that the earth is *not only* an object of idealist representation he concedes, at least implicitly, that idealist representation plays some role in standing.

7. It is interesting and important to note that in section 3 of *Totality and Infinity* Levinas joins this description of consciousness—that is, as perpetual postponement, as not yet—to the relationship of language, specifically to the role language plays in objectification.

> Objectification is produced [*se produit*] in the very work of language, where the subject is detached from the things possessed as though it hovered over its own existence, as though it were detached from it, as though the existence it exists had not yet [*ne . . . était pas encore*] completely reached it. This distance is more radical than every distance in the world. The subject must find itself "at a distance" [«*à distance*»] from its own being, even with regard to that taking distance that is inherent in the home, by which it is still in being. For negation remains within the totality, even when it bears upon the totality of the world. In order that objective distance be hollowed out, it is necessary that while in being

the subject be not yet in being [*n'y soit pas encore*], that in a certain sense it be not yet [*ne soit pas encore*] born—that it not be in nature. If the subject capable of objectivity *is* not yet [*n'est pas encore*] completely, this "not yet" [*«pas encore»*], this state of potency relative to act, does not denote a less than being, but denotes time. Consciousness of the object—thematization—rests on distance with regard to oneself, which can only be time; or, if one prefers, it rests on self-consciousness, if we recognize the "distance from self to self" in self-consciousness to be "time." However, time can designate a "not yet" [*«pas encore»*] that nevertheless would not be a "lesser being"—it can remain distant both from being and from death—only as the inexhaustible future of infinity, that is, as what is produced [*se produit*] in the very relationship of language. (TeI 184–85/TaI 209–10)

Language—like consciousness, insofar as it is not yet—is itself, as pointed out in chapter 1, the relation without relation of the subject and the other.

It is important to note that the phrases *at a distance* and *not yet* in this passage refer, among other things, to Levinas's reading of Descartes' *Meditations* (see especially TeI 25/TaI 54). In fact, Levinas's reading of Descartes' *Meditations* plays a significant role in the paragraphs immediately following the paragraph within which this passage is located.

4. ON THE GENEALOGY OF DEATH

1. David Farrell Krell, *Daimon Life: Heidegger and Life-Philosophy* (Bloomington: Indiana University Press, 1992), 246.

2. A few pages later, within the context of the certitude/indefiniteness of death considered earlier and reversing the order of presentation, Heidegger wonders: "How does the anticipatory understanding project itself upon a potentiality-for-Being which is certain and which is constantly possible in such a way that the 'when' in which the utter impossibility of existence becomes possible remains constantly indefinite?" (SZ 265/BT 310).

3. John Sallis, *Echoes: After Heidegger* (Bloomington: Indiana University Press, 1990), 130, emphasis added.

4. Ibid.

5. See Paul Davies, "A Fine Risk: Reading Blanchot Reading Levinas," in *Re-Reading Levinas*, 201–26, ed. Robert Bernasconi and Simon Critchley (Bloomington: Indiana University Press, 1991).

6. See also Blanchot's *The Writing of the Disaster*:

I cannot welcome the Other, not even with an acceptance that would be infinite. Such is the new and difficult feature of the plot. The other, as neighbor, is the relation that I cannot sustain, and whose approach is death itself, the mortal proximity (he who sees God dies: for "dying" is one manner of seeing the invisible, of saying the ineffable. Dying is the indiscretion wherein God, become somehow and necessarily a god without truth, surrenders to passivity). (ED 42/WD 23)

In both cases, see Exodus 33:18–23.

> Moses said, "I pray thee, show me thy glory." And he said, "I will make all my goodness pass before you, and will proclaim before you my name 'The LORD'; and I will be gracious to whom I will be gracious, and will show mercy on whom I will show mercy. But," he said, "you cannot see my face; for man shall not see me and live." And the LORD said, "Behold, there is a place by me where you shall stand upon the rock; and while my glory passes by I will put you in a cleft of the rock, and I will cover you with my hand until I have passed by; then I will take away my hand, and you shall see my back; but my face shall not be seen." (Exodus 33:18–23, Revised Standard Version)

It is interesting to note that Levinas refers to this passage from the Bible in his early articulations of the logic of the "trace" (see "Meaning and Sense" and "The Trace of the Other"). It is also interesting to note that a few lines after Blanchot writes, "Whoever sees God dies" (and within the same paragraph) he uses the term *trace*:

> *I say a flower*! But in the absence where I mention it, through the oblivion to which I relegate the image it gives me, in the depths of this heavy word, itself looming up like an unknown thing, I passionately summon the darkness of this flower, I summon this perfume that passes through me though I do not breathe it, this dust that impregnates me though I do not see it, this color which is a trace and not light. (LDM 316/LRD 46)

      7. Here, perhaps, is Zarathustra's "experience" of death as the impossibility of dying.

      8. Including the affirmation of the overman: nothingness.

      9. Levinas's remarks on death in *Totality and Infinity* seem to relegate it to a position that is superseded by suffering. For example: "The supreme ordeal of the will is not death, but suffering" (TeI 216/TaI 239). I would suggest that this passage reflects a particular reading of death, that is, death as nothingness. This reading, which Levinas sometimes associates with the work of Heidegger, is tempered by Levinas's earlier description of death as situated *between* being and nothingness in the interval of the not yet.

5. RESPONSIBILITY: REREADING "ON THE GENEALOGY OF DEATH"

      1. Despite the proximity of Heidegger to Patočka, the differences between them (Derrida notes) are significant: "The theme of authenticity, the links among care, being-towards-death, freedom, and responsibility, the very idea of a genesis or a history of

egological subjectivity, all such ideas certainly have a Heideggerian flavor to them. But this genealogy is hardly Heideggerian in style when it takes into account an incorporation of an earlier mystery that blurs the limits of every epoch" (DM 26/GD 19).

2. Before proceeding, however, it should be pointed out that while the parallel with Heidegger can be extended (with certain reservations that Derrida notes, DM 37–39, 45, 55/GD 31–33, 41–42, 52) to Heidegger's analysis of being-responsible or being-guilty (*Schuldigsein*), I propose to focus on Heidegger's analysis of death, especially as it is read by Derrida in *Aporias*.

3. The term *justice* here seems to indicate that which exceeds justice understood as a universal principle. The term undergoes slippage in this passage insofar as it summons me to go beyond justice understood as a universal principle. In that part of *Otherwise than Being* titled "From Saying to the Said, or the Wisdom of Desire" Levinas writes: "Signification signifies in justice, but also, more ancient than itself and than the equality implied by it, justice passes by justice in my responsibility for the other, in my inequality with respect to him for whom I am a hostage" (AE 201/OB 158). On the one hand, signification, the one-for-the-other of responsibility, signifies or leaves a trace of itself in the said, in the order of justice. It leaves a trace of itself in its interruption of this order. On the other hand, justice passes by justice, that is, in the judgment of God or justice that "summons me to respond," that is "addressed to an infinite responsibility" (TeI 222/TaI 244), one is summoned (given the aporetic character of responsibility) to go beyond justice understood as a universal principle. Responsibility signifies or leaves a trace of itself in the order of justice; the order of justice, as the site of this trace of responsibility, signifies responsibility.

4. See Paul Davies, "A Linear Narrative? Blanchot with Heidegger in the Work of Levinas," in *Philosophers' Poets*, 37–69, ed. David Wood (London: Routledge, 1990).

5. This passage parallels the inversion from the fear of death into the fear of committing murder considered in *Totality and Infinity*, which, for Levinas, is a formulation of death as possibility turning into death as impossibility.

6. In fact, according to Levinas's reading of Nemo's interpretation of Job, this is how Nemo would read this passage (despite the exceptional relationship he sets up between the soul and evil). Therefore, according to Levinas, in this instance, Nemo and the tradition are agreed.

7. See Jean-Luc Marion, "Metaphysics and Phenomenology: A Relief for Theology," trans. Thomas A. Carlson, *Critical Inquiry* 20 (Summer 1994): 590n35.

8. Although the Platonic mystery is preserved in the Christian mystery in its repression of the Platonic mystery, what is the status of the Platonic mystery in the Christian mystery? Recall that Levinas identifies Plato's idea of the "good existing beyond being (*agathon epekeina tes ousias*)" as a trace of the ethical breaking through the ontological (DEL 25).

9. Derrida expands the list of other others to include not only other persons, but also "places, animals, languages" (DM 70/GD 71).

Select Bibliography

WORKS BY EMMANUEL LEVINAS

L'au-delà du verset: Lectures et discours talmudiques. Paris: Minuit, 1982 / *Beyond the Verse: Talmudic Readings and Lectures*. Translated by Gary D. Mole. Bloomington: Indiana University Press, 1994.

Autrement qu'être ou au-delà de l'essence. Dordrecht: Kluwer, 1991 / *Otherwise than Being or Beyond Essence*. Translated by Alphonso Lingis. The Hague: Martinus Nijhoff, 1981.

De l'existence à l'existant. Paris: Vrin, 1990 / *Existence and Existents*. Translated by Alphonso Lingis. The Hague: Martinus Nijhoff, 1978.

"Dialogue with Emmanuel Levinas." Translated by Richard Kearney. In *Face to Face with Levinas*, 13–33. Edited by Richard A. Cohen. Albany: State University of New York Press, 1986.

"Dieu et la philosophie." In *De Dieu qui vient à l'idée*, 2nd ed., 93–127. Paris: Vrin, 1992 / "God and Philosophy." Translated by Alphonso Lingis and Richard Cohen. In *Emmanuel Levinas: Collected Philosophical Papers*, 153–73. Dordrecht: Martinus Nijhoff, 1987.

Difficile liberté: Essais sur le judaïsme, 2nd ed. Paris: Albin Michel, 1963 and 1976 / *Difficult Freedom: Essays on Judaism*. Translated by Seán Hand. Baltimore: The Johns Hopkins University Press, 1990.

Du sacré au saint: Cinq nouvelles lectures talmudiques. Paris: Minuit, 1977 / *From the Sacred to the Holy: Five New Talmudic Readings*. In *Nine Talmudic Readings*, 89–197. Translated by Annette Aronowicz. Bloomington: Indiana University Press, 1990.

La mort et le temps. Paris: Éditions de l'Herne, 1991.

"Mourir pour . . ." In *Heidegger: Questions ouvertes*, 255–64. Paris: Osiris, 1988.

"Notes sur le sens." In *De Dieu qui vient à l'idée*, 2nd ed., 231–57. Paris: Vrin, 1992.

"La philosophie et l'idée de l'Infini." In *En découvrant l'existence avec Husserl et Heidegger*, 165–78. Paris: Vrin, 1967 / "Philosophy and the Idea of Infinity." Translated by Alphonso Lingis. In *Emmanuel Levinas: Collected Philosophical Papers*, 47–59. Dordrecht: Martinus Nijhoff, 1987.

"La signification et le sens." In *Humanisme de l'autre homme*, 15–70. Montpellier: Fata Morgana, 1972 / "Meaning and Sense." Translated by Alphonso Lingis. In *Emmanuel Levinas: Collected Philosophical Papers*, 75–107. Dordrecht: Martinus Nijhoff, 1987.

"La souffrance inutile." In *Les Cahiers de La nuit surveillée, Numéro 3; Emmanuel Levinas*, 329–38. Edited by Jacques Rolland. Paris: Éditions Verdier, 1984 / "Useless Suffering." Translated by Richard Cohen. In *The Provocation of Levinas: Rethinking the Other*, 156–67. Edited by Robert Bernasconi and David Wood. London: Routledge, 1988.

Le temps et l'autre. Paris: PUF, 1991 / *Time and the Other*. Translated by Richard A. Cohen. Pittsburgh: Duquesne University Press, 1991.

Théorie de l'intuition dans la phénoménologie de Husserl, 5th ed. Paris: Vrin, 1984 / *The Theory of Intuition in Husserl's Phenomenology*. Translated by André Orianne. Evanston: Northwestern University Press, 1973.

Totalité et Infini: Essai sur l'extériorité, 4th ed. The Hague: Martinus Nijhoff, 1984 / *Totality and Infinity: An Essay on Exteriority*. Translated by Alphonso Lingis. Pittsburgh: Duquesne University Press, 1969.

"La trace de l'autre." In *En découvrant l'existence avec Husserl et Heidegger*, 187–202. Paris: Vrin, 1967 / "The Trace of the Other." Translated by Alphonso Lingis. In *Deconstruction in Context: Literature and Philosophy*, 345–59. Edited by Mark C. Taylor. Chicago: University of Chicago Press, 1986.

"Transcendance et Mal." In *De Dieu qui vient à l'idée*, 2nd ed., 189–207. Paris: Vrin, 1992 / "Transcendence and Evil." Translated by Alphonso Lingis. In *Emmanuel Levinas: Collected Philosophical Papers*, 175–86. Dordrecht: Martinus Nijhoff, 1987.

OTHER WORKS

Bernasconi, Robert. "Rereading *Totality and Infinity*." In *The Question of the Other*, 23–34. Edited by Arleen Dallery and Charles Scott. Albany: State University of New York Press, 1989.

————. "The Silent Anarchic World of the Evil Genius." In *The Collegium Phaenom-enologicum: The First Ten Years*, 257–72. Edited by John C. Sallis, Giuseppina Moneta, and Jacques Taminiaux. Dordrecht: Martinus Nijhoff, 1988.

————. "Skepticism in the Face of Philosophy." In *Re-Reading Levinas*, 149–61. Edited by Robert Bernasconi and Simon Critchley. Bloomington: Indiana University Press, 1991.

Blanchot, Maurice. *La communauté inavouable*. Paris. Minuit, 1983 / *The Unavowable Community*. Translated by Pierre Joris. Barrytown, New York: Station Hill Press, 1988.

————. *L'écriture du désastre*. Paris: Gallimard, 1980 / *The Writing of the Disaster*. Translated by Ann Smock. Lincoln: University of Nebraska Press, 1986.

————. *L'entretien infini*. Paris: Gallimard, 1969 / *The Infinite Conversation*. Translated by Susan Hanson. Minneapolis: University of Minnesota Press, 1993.

————. *L'espace littéraire*. Paris: Gallimard, 1955 / *The Space of Literature*. Translated by Ann Smock. Lincoln: University of Nebraska Press, 1982.

————. "La littérature et le droit à la mort." In *La part du feu*, 291–331. Paris: Gallimard, 1949 / "Literature and the Right to Death." Translated by Lydia Davis. In *The Gaze of Orpheus*, 21–62. Edited by P. Adams Sitney. Barrytown, New York: Station Hill Press, 1981.

————. *Le pas au-delà*. Paris: Gallimard, 1973 / *The Step Not Beyond*. Translated by Lycette Nelson. Albany: State University of New York Press, 1992.

Critchley, Simon. *The Ethics of Deconstruction*. Oxford: Blackwell, 1992.

Davies, Paul. "The Face and the Caress: Levinas's Ethical Alterations of Sensibility." In *Modernity and the Hegemony of Vision*, 252–72. Edited by David Michael Levin. Berkeley: University of California Press, 1993.

————. "A Fine Risk: Reading Blanchot Reading Levinas." In *Re-Reading Levinas*, 201–26. Edited by Robert Bernasconi and Simon Critchley. Bloomington: Indiana University Press, 1991.

————. "A Linear Narrative? Blanchot with Heidegger in the Work of Levinas." In *Philosophers' Poets*, 37–69. Edited by David Wood. London: Routledge, 1990.

————. "On Resorting to an Ethical Language." In *Ethics as First Philosophy: The Significance of Emmanuel Levinas for Philosophy, Literature and Religion*, 95–104. Edited by Adriaan T. Peperzak. New York: Routledge, 1995.

de Vries, Hent. "Adieu, à dieu, a-Dieu." In *Ethics as First Philosophy: The Significance of Emmanuel Levinas for Philosophy, Literature and Religion*, 211–20. Edited by Adriaan T. Peperzak. New York: Routledge, 1995.

Derrida, Jacques, *Apories: Mourir—s'attendre aux «limites de la vérité.»* In *Le passage des frontières: Autour du travail de Jacques Derrida*, 309–38. Paris:

Galilée, 1994 / *Aporias: Dying—Awaiting (One Another at) the "Limits of Truth."* Translated by Thomas Dutoit. Stanford: Stanford University Press, 1993.

———. *De la grammatologie.* Paris: Minuit, 1967 / *Of Grammatology.* Translated by Gayatri Chakravorty Spivak. Baltimore: Johns Hopkins University Press, 1976.

———. *Donner la mort.* In *L'éthique du don, Jacques Derrida et la pensée du don,* 11–108. Paris: Métailié-Transition, 1992 / *The Gift of Death.* Translated by David Wills. Chicago: University of Chicago Press, 1995.

———. *L'écriture et la différence.* Paris: Seuil, 1967 / *Writing and Difference.* Translated by Alan Bass. Chicago: University of Chicago Press, 1978.

———. *Mémoires pour Paul de Man.* Paris: Galilée, 1988 / *Memoires for Paul de Man.* Translated by Cecile Lindsay, Jonathan Culler, and Eduardo Cadava. New York: Columbia University Press, 1986.

———. *Points . . . : Interviews, 1974–1994.* Translated by Peggy Kamuf & others. Edited by Elisabeth Weber. Stanford: Stanford University Press, 1995.

Descartes, René. *Meditationes de prima philosophia.* In *Oeuvres de Descartes,* vol. VII, 1–90. Edited by Charles Adam and Paul Tannery. Paris: Vrin, 1983 / *Meditations on First Philosophy.* Translated by John Cottingham. In *The Philosophical Writings of Descartes,* vol. II, 1–62. Cambridge: Cambridge University Press, 1988.

Hegel, G. W. F., *Phänomenologie des Geistes.* Edited by Wolfgang Bonsiepen and Reinhard Heede. In *Gesammelte Werke,* Bd. 9. Hamburg: Felix Meiner Verlag, 1980 / *Phenomenology of Spirit.* Translated by A. V. Miller. Oxford: Oxford University Press, 1977.

Heidegger, Martin. *Sein und Zeit,* 9th ed. Tübingen: Max Niemeyer, 1960 / *Being and Time.* Translated by John Macquarrie and Edward Robinson. New York: Harper & Row, 1962.

Kierkegaard, Søren. *Frygt og Bæven: Dialektisk Lyrik.* In *Søren Kierkegaards Samlede Værker,* vol. III. Edited by A. B. Drachman, J. L. Heiberg, and H. O. Lange. Copenhagen: Gyldendal, 1901–06 / *Fear and Trembling: Dialectical Lyric.* Edited and Translated by Howard V. Hong and Edna H. Hong. Princeton: Princeton University Press, 1983.

Krell, David Farrell. *Daimon Life: Heidegger and Life-Philosophy.* Bloomington: Indiana University Press, 1992.

Llewelyn, John. *Emmanuel Levinas: The Genealogy of Ethics.* London: Routledge, 1995.

Marion, Jean-Luc. "Metaphysics and Phenomenology: A Relief for Theology." Translated by Thomas A. Carlson. *Critical Inquiry* 20 (Summer 1994): 572–91.

Nancy, Jean-Luc. *La communauté désœuvrée*. Paris: Christian Bourgois Editeur, 1986 / *The Inoperative Community*. Translated by Peter Connor, Lisa Garbus, Michael Holland, and Simona Sawhney. Minneapolis: University of Minnesota Press, 1991.

Nietzsche, Friedrich. *Also sprach Zarathustra: Ein Buch für Alle und Keinen*. In *Werke: Kritische Gesamtausgabe*, Abt. VI, Bd. 1. Edited by Giorgio Colli and Mazzino Montinari. Berlin: Walter de Gruyter, 1968 / *Thus Spoke Zarathustra: A Book for All and None*. Translated by Walter Kaufmann. New York: Penguin, 1978.

———.*Nachgelassene Fragmente*. In *Werke: Kritische Gesamtausgabe*, Abt. VIII, Bd. 1. Edited by Giorgio Colli and Mazzino Montinari. Berlin: Walter de Gruyter, 1974 / *The Will to Power*. Translated by Walter Kaufmann and R. J. Hollingdale. New York: Random House, 1967.

———.*Zur Genealogie der Moral: Eine Streitschrift*. In *Werke: Kritische Gesamtausgabe*, Abt. VI, Bd. 2. Edited by Giorgio Colli and Mazzino Montinari. Berlin: Walter de Gruyter, 1968 / *On the Genealogy of Morals: A Polemic*. Translated by Walter Kaufmann. New York: Random House, 1967.

Patočka, Jan. "Je technická civilizace úpadková, a proč?," In *Kacířské eseje o filosofii dějin*, 105–26. Praha: Academia, 1990 / "Is Technological Civilization Decadent, and Why?" Translated by Erazim Kohák. In *Heretical Essays in the Philosophy of History*, 95–118. Edited by James Dodd. Chicago: Open Court, 1996.

Sallis, John. *Echoes: After Heidegger*. Bloomington: Indiana University Press, 1990.

Wahl, Jean. *Petite histoire de "l'existentialisme."* Paris: Éditions Club Maintenant, 1947 / *A Short History of Existentialism*. Translated by Forrest Williams and Stanley Maron. New York: Philosophical Library, 1949.

Index

A

Abraham, 105; Kierkegaard and Derrida on, 4, 99–101; Levinas on, 58, 95, 97–98

à-Dieu, 3, 4, 31, 94, 103, 104–105

B

Bernasconi, Robert, 7, 107n2

Blanchot, Maurice, 1–2, 20, 69, 78; on community, 105; on dead time, 107n3; on double death, 57, 59; on God, 112n6; on Hegel, 47–49, 58–63; on Heidegger, 47–49, 51–53, 57, 76, 80; on literature, 59–63; on Nietzsche, 48–49, 63–66; on Reign of Terror, 62; on responsibility, 77, 79, 85, 92; on revolution, 59–63

by-the-other/for-the-other, 44, 68, 81–82

C

Christian mystery, 69–70, 72, 91, 114n8

Christianity, 72–78, 88–92, 96, 98, 102

community, 104–106

contradiction, 23–31

D

Davies, Paul, 81, 112n5, 114n4

dead time: definition of, 2

demonic/orgiastic mystery, 69–71, 91

Derrida, Jacques, 1–2, 20, 33, 49, 107n1; on dead time, 107n3; on Heidegger, 51–57, 70–78, 88–92, 99, 101, 104, 113n1, 114n2; on Kierkegaard, 3, 98–102, 114n9; on Patočka, 69–75, 77–78, 88–92, 96, 98, 102, 113n1

Descartes, René, 2–3, 5–18, 20–24, 28–31, 32–39, 44, 46, 54, 67, 81, 84, 86, 87–88, 92–93, 102–103, 105, 108n4, 108n5, 109n2, 110n5, 111n7

double origin: definition of, 5, 10

doubt, 2, 14–17, 22–24, 31, 80

dwelling, 35–42, 67–68, 110n6

E

elemental, 34–43, 110n6

Eliot, T.S., 106

enjoyment, 34–37, 40–44, 109n2, 110n3

evil, 83–88, 114n6